Edward A. Warren

SPARTAN EDUCATION

By EDWARD H. WARREN

THE LAWBOOK EXCHANGE, LTD.
Clark, New Jersey

ISBN 978-1-58477-585-0 (hardcover)
ISBN 978-1-61619-100-9 (paperback)

Lawbook Exchange edition 2005, 2013

The quality of this reprint is equivalent to the quality of the original work.

THE LAWBOOK EXCHANGE, LTD.

33 Terminal Avenue
Clark, New Jersey 07066-1321

*Please see our website for a selection of our other publications
and fine facsimile reprints of classic works of legal history:*
www.lawbookexchange.com

Library of Congress Cataloging-in-Publication Data

Warren, Edward H. (Edward Henry), 1873-1945.
  Spartan education / Edward H. Warren.
    p. cm.
  Originally published: Boston : Houghton Mifflin Co., 1942.
  Includes bibliographical references and index.
  ISBN 1-58477-585-8 (alk. paper)
1. Law--Study and teaching--United States. 2. Warren, Edward H.
(Edward Henry), 1873-1945. 3. Law teachers--Massachusetts--
Biography. 4. Harvard Law School--History. I. Title.

KF273.W365 2005
340'.071'17444--dc22   2004024270

Printed in the United States of America on acid-free paper

SPARTAN
EDUCATION

By EDWARD H. WARREN

HOUGHTON MIFFLIN COMPANY · BOSTON

The Riverside Press Cambridge

1942

DEDICATED
TO
THE HARVARD LAW SCHOOL

Contents

Preface

I SHALL BE SEVENTY next January, and that is a good time to call it a day. When a man's sun sinks below the western horizon and the twilight hours begin, it is natural for him to review his life, to philosophize and reminisce. Hence this little book.

My life has been many-sided. I should like to be remembered as a teacher. Time was, when I winced at that description (page 11), but I have come to regard it as a most honorable title. I should be glad to see more young men who are really first-class adopt education as their life work. In Chapter II, I have sought to give some helpful suggestions to younger men who earnestly seek to justify their existence by becoming effective teachers of the law.

I believe in discipline. From boyhood days on, I have sought to discipline my own mind, pen, and tongue. And throughout my service on the Law Faculty I have sought to discipline the minds, pens, and tongues of the students. I have never suffered fools gladly, and regard such sufferance as mischievous. Therefore 'Spartan Education' seemed an appropriate title.

As I review my life, I find the source of greatest satisfaction in my belief that there are today ten thousand men who are leading more useful and successful lives than they would be leading if my Spartan training had not played a substantial part in the moulding of their minds; and that most, if not all, of them now recognize that to be the fact, and are grateful.

The book is not without its crusading aspects. At pages 44–49 I have given free expression to my thoughts on the war. And in Chapter III, I have sought to sound the bugle for an assault upon the present literary style (or lack of literary style) of many jurists on and off the bench; in Chapters IV, V, and VI, I have sought to supplement precept by example, and to demonstrate by a few specific examples that the best way to be persuasive is to be simple, clear, and terse.

During the years I have prepared four case books, — Cases on Corporations, first edition of 1909 and second edition of 1916, and Cases on Property, first edition of 1915 and second edition of 1938 (all of which were manufactured by The Riverside Press, Cambridge, Massachusetts). I have written two treatises, — one on *Corporate Advantages Without Incorporation* (which was pub-

lished in 1929 by Baker, Voorhis and Company, New York City)
and one on *Margin Customers* (which was in 1941 manufactured
and is now being distributed by The Plimpton Press, Norwood,
Massachusetts). In 1915 I drafted a series of laws concerning
corporations which, with some modifications, were enacted by
the General Assembly of the State of Vermont. Soon after joining the Harvard Law Faculty in 1904, I undertook, at the
request of Mr. John C. Gray (who was too busy to do it himself),
to write for the Cyclopaedia of Law and Procedure an exposition
of the Rule against Perpetuities and the Suspension of the Power
of Alienation which will be found in 30 Cyc. 1464–1525. I have
also written about a dozen law review articles which are inventoried in the footnote.[1] And I have written numerous
opinions, briefs, wills, corporate organization and reorganization
papers, and business contracts. I estimate that the total of all
these various matters would exceed ten thousand printed pages.

[1] Collateral Attack on Incorporation. A. De Facto Corporations. 20 *Harvard
Law Review*, pp. 456–480 (April, 1907).

Collateral Attack on Incorporation. B. In General. 21 *Harvard Law Review*, pp.
305–331 (March, 1908).

Executed Ultra Vires Transactions. 23 *Harvard Law Review*, pp. 495–512 (May,
1910).

Executory Ultra Vires Transactions. 24 *Harvard Law Review*, pp. 534–547 (May,
1911).

Welter of Decisions. 10 *Illinois Law Review*, pp. 472–478 (February, 1916).
See pp. 79–85 of this book.

Voluntary Transfers of Corporate Undertakings. 30 *Harvard Law Review*, pp. 335–
366 (February, 1917).

Taxability of Stock Dividends as Income. 33 *Harvard Law Review*, pp. 885–901
(May, 1920).

The Progress of the Law, 1919–1920: Corporations. 34 *Harvard Law Review*,
pp. 282–308 (January, 1921).

Safeguarding the Creditors of Corporations. 36 *Harvard Law Review*, pp. 509–547
(March, 1923).

Torts by Corporations in Ultra Vires Undertakings. 2 *Cambridge* (England)
Law Journal, pp. 180–191 (1925).

Qualifying as Plaintiff in an Action for a Conversion. 49 *Harvard Law Review*,
pp. 1084–1109 (May, 1936).

A Book Review; the Law of Future Interests. 2 *Toronto Law Journal*, pp. 389–
392 (1937).

A Problem in Tacking. 88 *Pennsylvania Law Review*, pp. 897–914 (June, 1940).

Serjeants-at-Law; the Order of the Coif. *Virginia Law Review*, May, 1942. See
pp. 108–144 of this book.

Bank of Seattle *v.* Gidden; a Reply to Samuel Williston. *Chicago Law Review*,
June, 1942.

Only enough is given in this book to indicate scope and quality.

When I was writing *Corporate Advantages Without Incorporation*, I was assisted by Colin Ives, who had taken a very high rank in the School and had returned for a graduate year, half of which was to be work with me. One day, after handing back a draft of a chapter with his suggestions, he said: 'It is all there, and you have converted me. But it is so compact and closely reasoned that there is a headache in every page. Why don't you write the way you lecture?'

That treatise has had a substantial amount of influence with the courts, and many practising lawyers have written that they have found it helpful. But it is unquestionably a tough book. It was aimed at tip-top third-year students and I advise first-year students to leave it alone (except for the discussion of *Hibbs* v. *Brown* at pages 477–500, which may do them good). But *Margin Customers* was aimed at first-year students. I had never forgotten what Ives said, and, although I did not adopt his suggestion for the first treatise, I did for the second. *Margin Customers* is tough enough, but it is definitely less tough than *Corporate Advantages Without Incorporation* (to be, or not to be, a legal unit). The strain is eased from time to time and that is primarily due to Ives (who is now going strong as a lawyer in New York City and whom I shall always retain in grateful remembrance).

I wish to acknowledge here the valuable assistance given with respect to this book by my secretary, Mrs. Commons. She has aided me by some very intelligent, helpful suggestions about the form of the new matter. And I am placing upon her, and she is accepting, sole responsibility (*a*) for preparing an accurate table of contents; (*b*) for preparing an accurate and adequate index; and (*c*) for seeing the book through the press.

E. H. W.

HARVARD LAW SCHOOL
June 1942

Your work has been unique and your fame as a
great teacher and master of the science of law has
extended throughout the English-speaking world.

President Conant to the author

Chapter One

THE INFLUENCES THAT MOULDED THE AUTHOR'S MIND

I PREPARED for Harvard at the Worcester High School, and was admitted in 1891 at the age of eighteen.

The bulk of the preparation was in courses in Latin, Greek, and Mathematics (there were other courses in English, French, History, and Physics). The instructors were all good, and two of them, William F. Abbot and Cary Field, who gave most of the Latin and Greek courses, were excellent.

From them I derived three invaluable things: (*a*) They encouraged me so to concentrate when I was studying that I should not, even for a single, discursive moment, think of anything whatever except the subject matter of the study. (*b*) They gave me an instinct for perfect accuracy, so that I became intolerant even of a misplaced accent. (*c*) They taught me never to be content with an English translation of Latin or Greek until I had found *just* the right word or expression to convey the thought of Caesar, Cicero, Ovid, Virgil, Xenophon, or Homer. I believe that there is no other way which is equally good for obtaining an adequate conception of the vast resources of the English language. I vividly remember how Mr. Abbot ignited my ambition by saying: 'Learn to be a sculptor in the English language.'

From 1891 to 1895 I was a Harvard undergraduate. In November, 1891, Dean Briggs gave an hour examination in English A, in which each student was directed to write an essay of about one page in length on a specified topic. Later, he spoke to the class of the results of that examination, and read my essay as the one that had pleased him most. I was delighted. Back in my room (19 Matthews), I told my roommate, who had prepared at a well-known preparatory school. 'For Heaven's sake,' he cried, 'keep that dark; it would kill you if it were known.'

At that time students were usually classified (by their fellow students) as Sports or Grinds. It was definitely *not* fashionable to study. The authorship of that essay remained a dark secret; only after the lapse of half a century do I dare to reveal it.

The desire of social recognition was more controlling among most of the students in Harvard in my time than any other desire. I suspect that that is still true, not only in Harvard, but in most other colleges at the present time. And even many parents seem to be more interested in what clubs or fraternities their sons make than in the evidences of their intellectual progress.

Throughout my four college years (despise me, if you will) I kept the courses in a duly subordinate place. True it is, that two great men, Charles Franklin Dunbar and William James, stirred me to the depths in Economics and Psychology, and I did enough studying (in a more or less surreptitious way) to be Number Twenty-five in the twenty-five students in the class of '95 elected to the Phi Beta Kappa. But throughout those four years my chief interest was in other things than my courses.

At the Worcester High School practically all the boys took part in the weekly meetings of the three debating societies which then flourished. I had enjoyed my part in the Sumner Club, — it gave me my first training in oral persuasiveness. When I came to Harvard, I joined the Harvard Union. In our freshman year I was chosen to be one of the three representatives of Harvard in a debate with Yale at New Haven, and happened to be the first of the six speakers. The genial, witty Chauncey M. Depew presided and made an opening address which the packed house thoroughly relished. He concluded in these words: 'If I were a starter, I should say "Go"; if I were an umpire, I should say "Play Ball"; but, as it is, I say "Edward H. Warren of Harvard has the floor."' I took the floor, but no sheet was ever whiter than my face.

In the following year I was again a representative of Harvard in a debate with Yale, — this time in Sanders Theatre in Cambridge. By a vote of two to one the judges decided for Harvard (there had been no decision the year before by appointed judges). But after that I dropped out of oratorical contests.

I remember the Union with mixed feelings. Through the Union I came to know and respect several men, friendship with whom endured. These included James P. Hall, later Dean of Chicago Law School, and Francis G. Caffey, who is still going strong as a Federal Judge in New York City. But there was a disturbingly large number of the members who impressed me as stronger below the nose than above the nose. I do not think that the Harvard Union in those days merited an appraisal on an equality with either the Oxford Union or the Cambridge Union of that date.

It was the *Crimson*, the college daily paper, that proved to be, directly and indirectly, of the greatest educational value to me in the college years. I became a candidate in my freshman year. One morning the *Boston Herald* published a proposal on an educational matter by the president of another college. The ideas advanced seemed to me to run counter to the ideas of President Eliot. If I could only get an interview with President Eliot, I thought that the editors of the *Crimson* would give me full marks.

The President was not so inaccessible as legend has made him. He received me, not cordially but courteously. I stated the situation and asked: 'Have you any comments which the *Crimson* might publish?' 'No,' said he. Just that one word. Then silence; polar silence. I folded my tent like the Arab.

But I was not going to leave it at that. I analyzed the statement of the other president, and framed eight pertinent questions to each of which a 'Yes' or 'No' answer might fairly be expected. I returned to the President, apologized for not having presented more definitely the points on which the readers of the *Crimson* would wish to be informed, and asked for the privilege of reading eight specific questions to which a 'Yes' or 'No' answer might be given. 'You may read them,' he said. I read question Number One. 'The answer to that is "No."' So on through the eight. When I had finished, President Eliot first smiled, then laughed.

That broke the ice. And the water under the ice was surprisingly warm. From that time on throughout the college years I was frequently received by him, usually in his office, but sometimes in his home. I doubt if any other ninety-five man (not related to him by blood or connected by marriage) saw so much of him.

His example did more to mould my mind than anything else has ever done. The cordial relations always continued. He was an extraordinary man. He was the embodiment of poise. I feel sure that he would have been serene with the Emperor of the Russias on the one hand and the Pope on the other hand. He was broadminded, with a vast amount of detailed information, shrewd, and wise. As an embodiment of dignity, intellect, and character I have never met his like in the flesh. He stands out in my memories as a noble rock, unshaken, undiminished, by the waves of controversy which broke upon him from time to time.

It is looking ahead beyond the college days, but out of the many things I have heard him say, I wish to quote three: 'Young men are of two kinds. If you give a young man something to do, one kind will in due time return with the thing done; the other kind will in due time return with some perfectly good reason why it cannot be done.' 'The most secure security is the unsecured promise of a high-grade educational institution.' 'The finest of the fine arts is to make a persuasive exposition by the written or spoken word.'

I prize my associations with President Eliot more than any other associations that I have ever had (barring, of course, associations with my parents, my wife, and my daughter).

In time I made the *Crimson*, and later became the head of the ninety-five board. While I was managing editor, Professor Charles Eliot Norton became interested in having certain letters of James Russell Lowell reach all, or at least the bulk, of the students, and he asked the *Crimson* to cooperate. I confess that I derived little benefit from his lectures on Fine Arts (a snap course), but the Lowell letters took me often to his study on Shady Hill, and it was through such contact with him that I obtained at least a dim conception of the possibilities of culture.

My position on the *Crimson* brought me into pleasant relations with a large number of my classmates. One of these, Robert D. (Bob) Wrenn, noted as a football, baseball, and tennis player, proved to be years later my first client. Another classmate was Robert Walcott, who, when he was later appointed a Justice in the Cambridge District Court, was the youngest Judge on the Bench in Massachusetts. His father, Doctor Walcott, a member of the Corporation, and at one time Acting President, always reminded me of a Roman Senator. More than once I was asked to take a meal in their home on Waterhouse Street (which I recently, with a pang, saw pulled down), and I have never forgotten the kindly interest which Doctor Walcott took in me (or the searching questions which he asked about undergraduate conditions).

In the senior year, each class meets (or, in those days, did meet) to elect Class Day officers and the permanent officers of the class. The Committee on Arrangements asked me to preside. At that meeting I was unanimously chosen to give the oration on Class Day, and that pleased me; half a century ago the word 'orator' did not have the connotations of splurge and gas that it now very frequently has.

President Eliot had just finished twenty-five years of service as President, and in the oration or address which I made in Sanders Theatre on Class Day, I tried to avoid the usual platitudes and to give cubical contents to the address by making it, in the main, an exposition of President Eliot's Harvard accomplishments during that quarter of a century.

What to do after college? My father wanted me to go on to the Law School, and many of my classmates did so. But the idea did not appeal to me. Sociology seemed to me the coming subject, and I resolved to fit myself to become a professor in Sociology. I secured an appointment as an instructor in New York University and in the year 1895–96 gave three courses (in the new buildings on University Heights), — one in History, one in Economics, and one in Sociology (nothing but the Statute of Limitations ever gave me a defense for some of the things that I said in that course). During the same year I spent about half of my time in studying Sociology and Economics in the Columbia Graduate School, and at the end of the year was given the degree of Master of Arts.

In 1896–97, I studied Economics in the Harvard Graduate School. I had become less enthusiastic, more dubious, about the possibilities of sociology. During that year Professor Taussig published a treatise on *Wages and Capital*, and at his request I prepared and gave two lectures in exposition of this treatise to my fellow students in Economics II, the advanced course in Economic Theory. In the spring of 1897, Professor Dunbar suddenly fell ill, and I took on and completed his course on the Financial History of the United States, meeting the class about fifteen times.

But just as I had moved from sociology to the more solid economics, so I moved from economics to the more solid law. At long last, I entered the Law School.

Then followed three most fruitful years, — fruitful for two reasons. When I was graduated from Harvard, my father, who had a competency, was prepared to pay my expenses as a student in the Law School. But I had declined that kindly offer, had gone my own (mistaken) way, and I did not like to go back to him and ask him to renew it. So I worked my way through the Law School, and am very glad that I had that experience. It taught me the value of a dollar, — it developed a canny streak in me. It also gave me a basis for a sympathetic understanding of other students who are up against it in financial matters, and who do not just lie down and moan.

And the very work by which I earned money trained my mind. I did all kinds of things. (a) I was one of the assistants in Economics I. (b) Dean Briggs put me in charge of certain undergraduates who were hopelessly floundering; I did not tutor them myself (engaging special tutors if necessary), but I showed them how to study, and by daily reports saw to it that they were studying. (c) In the summer of 1898, and in the spring of 1899, I did straight tutoring in all the first-year law courses. (d) And I even gave lectures on Current Topics in certain fashionable schools in Boston for young ladies. Charming!

In these various ways I made in two years enough to support me for three, with a good balance to back me when I tackled New York City. And it was well that I had that balance, for in those days the New York offices paid (in the first year) little or nothing to recent Harvard Law School graduates, even if they had obtained tip-top grades at the School.

But these advantages were collateral, — not directly due to the School. What did the School do for me? I might better ask, What did the School not do for me? I fell in love with the School at first sight, and that love still abideth with me.

Comparisons are odious. I make no comparison of the School in 1897–1900 with the School in years before or in years after. I wish to speak of the School, not relatively, but absolutely.

To speak, first, of the Faculty. The Big Four, Thayer, Gray, Smith, and Ames, were all going strong. They were remarkable men, — every one of them.

Their qualities were in some respects dissimilar. Judge Smith overflowed with the milk of human kindness; he won the first place in my affections. He had had a large experience at the bar and on the bench in New Hampshire, was very shrewd, had an aptitude for simple, homely illustrations, and he had his feet right on the ground all the time.

I cannot resist diverting to tell a story which was Law School legend in our time. Judge Smith's father had as a boy served in the campaign against Burgoyne. After the war he had married and had a son, who had died while still young. The father married again and when he was over seventy Jeremiah was born. The legend was that one day Judge Smith came to the Law School, looking depressed. Dean Ames expressed his concern, and hoped that he was in no trouble. 'Just a hundred years ago today,' Judge Smith sadly said, 'my brother died.'

John Chipman Gray gave the three Property courses (one in each of the three years). He was a member of one of the large Boston firms and the solid men of Boston put a very high appraisal on his considered opinion on any property or business question. He was at the School two, sometimes three, days a week. He was master of his subject, and I do not recall that in the whole three years any man in our class was able to detect the slightest inaccuracy in his exposition of the authorities.

There was also a legend about him. A student came to put to him a question on a knotty point, and Mr. Gray was reported to have said: 'If you want to know what the law *was*, you should speak to Dean Langdell [Dean Langdell had ceased in our day to do much work with the students]; if you want to know what the law *will be*, you should speak to Dean Ames; but if you want to know what the law *is*, you may draw up your chair.'

James Bradley Thayer was also a very learned scholar, and his *Preliminary Treatise on the Law of Evidence* remains as a monument to his meticulously careful, indefatigable researches. He taught Evidence and Constitutional Law. The second subject calls for the qualities of a statesman, and he had those qualities. He was a very broad, well-balanced, farseeing man. A wise seer. He sowed seed in my mind which did not ripen until years later. The longer I live, the higher my appraisal of him goes.

Dean Ames was the most stimulating teacher of the four. He carried on his courses chiefly by means of Socratic dialogues between himself and fifteen or twenty of the best students who formed, so to speak, a Greek chorus. He had the art of sending us out of every class in a perfect turmoil of conflicting thoughts which usually did not wholly subside, even after long discussion among ourselves.

I can never be adequately grateful for what those four great men did in moulding my mind.

But not all that I gained in those three years from the School came from the members of the Faculty. The student body comprised the pick of the young legal brains in the country.

It was fashionable to work. Gone was the college distinction between Sports and Grinds. Over three quarters of the students worked hard. Sixty hours a week was common; seventy hours a week not infrequent.

The fellow students from whom I gained most by discussion out of class included Beekman Winthrop, Joseph Warren, Sydney Wrightington, Joseph H. Choate, Jr., and Dean Sage.

Dean Sage was a Yale man, but — believe it or believe it not — he was (and is) a very likeable person. He is now the head of one of the large New York firms and has also rendered such distinguished public service that both Yale and Columbia have conferred honorary degrees upon him. I have never found it easy to enter into an *intimate* friendship, but I have been so fortunate as to have had five intimate friends, and Sage was of the five. I saw a good deal of him in student days, and also in the four years when I practised law in New York. In the twenty-five years (1904–29) between my joining the Harvard Law Faculty and my going abroad to live, we never allowed anything to prevent us from dining together once a year, — sometimes I went to New York and sometimes he came to Boston. Those dinners were part of my (and his) education.

From 1900 to 1904, I practised law in New York City. But before I speak of those years, I wish to mention an incident in the spring of 1901 which nearly changed the current of my life. President Eliot was nearing seventy, and was carrying a great load. Some of the members of the Corporation and the Board of Overseers urged him to ease the load by delegating part of the work to a younger man. He wrote me offering the position. I was very much pleased, and my admiration for him was so profound that I was at first strongly inclined to accept. I travelled to Cambridge to speak with him about it and was received by him and Mrs. Eliot in the old president's house at 17 Quincy Street.

But on turning the matter over in my mind, I was inclined to doubt the wisdom of taking the position. I felt sure that so long as he continued to be President, I should have, in association with him, a rare opportunity and a delightful existence. But I did not see any satisfactory permanent future. I felt that I would on his retirement (which in fact occurred eight years later) be under the necessity of beginning life all over again, whereas if I continued in the law I could reasonably expect a satisfactory permanent future. For these reasons I ultimately decided to keep on in the law.

To return to the four years, 1900 to 1904, spent in the practice of the law in New York City. The men who during those four years did most to mould my mind were John L. Cadwalader, George W. Wickersham, Henry W. Taft, and Edward J. Hancy.

During the summer of 1898 I had tutored Frank Thomson, son of the President of the Pennsylvania Railroad, at their home in Merion, and it was through the Thomsons that I secured a place in Strong and Cadwalader. Soon after I had begun work, Mr. Cadwalader called me into his office, and inquired where my abode was, and where I was taking my dinners. He approved my arrangements, but then proceeded to say: 'You remind me of a tramp. [Pause.] The tramp was hungry, and he was looking up a tree where a fat coon lay. A passer-by said to him: "You can't catch him." "Stranger," said the tramp, "I got to."'

By good luck, a case came into the office involving a power of appointment, and Mr. Cadwalader directed me to draft the brief. I was fresh from Mr. Gray, the outstanding American authority on this topic, and my training under him enabled me to write a brief. Mr. Cadwalader made some changes, and directed me to file the brief, as amended, in the name of the firm, with his name and my name under his as counsel (although I had not been in the office above four months). That was very decent of him. It was not only pleasing, but also valuable to me, as about half a dozen of large New York firms were attorneys for different parties in interest.

Mr. Cadwalader was a *grand seigneur*. I dare say that he knew everybody whom he cared to know in New York, Philadelphia, and Washington. He was held in respect and awe by many of the old families. He was like the chieftain of a clan.

The firm was entrusted with the management of many estates, and a large income flowed in without the beneficiaries ever crossing the threshold of the office. Mr. Wickersham (later Attorney-General of the United States) and Mr. Taft (brother of President Taft) had attracted to the firm some important corporations, and they certainly worked a good deal harder than Mr. Cadwalader did. The time came when they felt that it would be equitable for them to receive a larger fraction of the firm's profits. They ventured to suggest this to Mr. Cadwalader. He promptly invited them to take dinner with him.

The appointments for the dinner were perfect. The foods were perfect. The wines were perfect. The service was perfect. The coffee, the brandy, the cigars were perfect. Mr. Cadwalader was charming. His stories of what had gone on behind the scenes in Washington when he was Assistant Secretary of State were fascinating. The hours sped away. Mr. Wickersham and Mr. Taft bade their host good-night. Not a word had been said about the division of the firm's profits.

Mr. Cadwalader's sarcasm was quiet, rapier-like, devastating. At times I exposed myself to it. It hurt. It hurt a lot. But I never made again the mistake that had provoked that bit of sarcasm. He revealed to me the beneficial, purging qualities of artistic sarcasm.

Mr. Cadwalader, Mr. Wickersham, and Mr. Taft were out-topped in sheer intellectual eminence by such men as James C. Carter and Joseph H. Choate. But all three were well within the charmed circle of the recognized leaders of the New York Bar. I repeat here what I said about them at page 223 of *Margin Customers:*

> All three men had both ideals and *also* the realistic approach to the task of implementing these ideals as a practical matter; they were insistent, with a Spartan insistence, upon absolute accuracy down to the minutest detail in getting at the facts which it was necessary to have in mind as a basis for a wise exercise of judgment.

I had always suspected that to be a highly successful lawyer one must be up to the tricks of the trade. Certainly there are in literature many, many passages where the thought is conveyed that a lawyer is one who makes the worse reason appear to be the better. And once a young, sweet thing (I note that President Roosevelt has lately, May, 1942, been ventriloquizing through one of the current crop) said to me: 'I could love a lawyer who can make black seem white.' There was nothing of that sort in Strong and Cadwalader. I believe that all the partners were decent by instinct. Anyway, they were always decent. I derived my code of legal ethics from them.

The cases in which I worked covered a great variety of subjects, including Contracts and Negotiable Instruments, but the bulk of the work was either in Property or in Corporations. About two thirds of the total was in Corporations.

Mr. Hancy was the head of the business, investing side of the firm, and was an extremely valuable, indispensable, part of the *tout ensemble*. He was the shrewdest man I have ever known. One summer when his wife and daughter were in Europe he asked me to live with him in his home, and talked very freely with me. His ideas about finance and investments were, *if and when seen*, simple (all perfect things are simple). In after years when I began to have money to invest, I followed the Hancy thoughts. And that was of inestimable value to me, for in the horrid 1929–32 years, when everything else was collapsing, over ninety per cent of those investments not only did not collapse but edged into higher ground.

Toward the close of my third year in the Law School, Dean Ames said that he was prepared to recommend my appointment as a member of the Faculty. I said that I knew of no position which would be more congenial to me, but that I thought that in my own case it would be better if I first seasoned myself by sweating blood in actual practice.

George Bernard Shaw has a line: 'Those who can't, teach.' From my youth I have been fascinated by effective teaching, but the thought expressed in that line of Shaw's had a large, deterrent influence. That is a characteristic Shaw quip, — half true, half misleading, wholly arresting.

It is true that many persons are attracted to teaching because that occupation gives them a sheltered life, and allows them, comfortably ensconced on shore, to enjoy the spectacle of ships struggling to survive in storm-tossed seas. During the year (1896–97) that I studied Economics in the Harvard Graduate School, I took a walk one afternoon with two fellow students and we fell to speaking of our ambitions. One man said in substance: 'Professors are parasites on society. I'm in this because it is the easiest way that I know of by which I can be supported'; and he smirked at his own astuteness. That disgusted me, and the incident had more than a little to do with my entering the Law School.

The effective teaching of youth is certainly vital, at least in a democracy. My ideal of democracy is that there should be a serious and sustained effort that equal opportunities (not equal *results*, but equal *opportunities*) should be given to all. The best should be at the helm (if that thought is aristocratic, make the most of it). But opportunities to *prove* themselves best should be made available to all. I do not see how a democracy can survive (in the Darwinian sense) unless in substance such is its ideal.

If that is the sound approach, then the importance to a nation of effective teaching looms very large. True it is, that experience cannot be transmitted. But young men and women *can* be trained so that they may come to know themselves, to find the work in life which they are best fitted to do well, and gradually to build their own lives profiting by foundations that have been laid by similar workers in the past. 'Educational' institutions which are used by a majority of the 'students' primarily for getting social recognition are luxuries which this nation, when at long last it emerges from the present multiple wars, will not be able to afford.

No man ought to be a teacher unless he undertakes the work, not because he is timid and craves an armchair, but because he thinks that he will find in teaching the opportunity for service for which *he* is best fitted.

In 1904, Judge Smith wanted to be relieved of part of the heavy load that he was carrying, and preferred that some younger man should take on the third-year course in Corporations. I was offered an appointment as an assistant professor in the Law School, with the understanding that I was to have sole charge of, and a free hand in, the course in Corporations, and that I should do such other work as might be assigned to me from time to time.

I accepted, and have never regretted that acceptance. I found my niche in life. For twenty-five years I gave the course in Corporations, and believe that I have never done anything else as well. At first I also gave the second-year course in Equity and a part of the second-year course in Property. Beginning with 1907, I gave the whole of the first-year course in Property, the whole of the second-year course in Property, and the whole of the third-year course in Corporations for many years. Happy years. Having the students year after year, I came really to know them and could, on meeting a third-year student in the street, usually (not always) call him by name.

I have found many congenial things about teaching. It is a pleasure to be within the four corners of a book and to commune with the great minds of the past. It is a pleasure to wrestle with a tough legal problem until at last the fundamentals are clearly seen. It is a pleasure to reduce thoughts to writing, fit in substance and in form to enable others to see what I have seen. Above all it is an exquisite pleasure to talk about the law (the charm of which age does not wither or custom stale) with groups of young men of good intellect who are intensely interested.

From 1904 to 1908, I devoted the whole of my time to preparing and giving my lectures, and familiarizing myself with the precedents from the dawn of the common law. In 1908, I opened an office in Boston for the practice of the law, and until 1921 was in town two or three days a week. This was done with the approval and encouragement of President Eliot. On broaching the matter to him, I found that he *wanted* me to do it. He said that he thought it was a distinct advantage to the Law School if at least some of the members of the Faculty gave part of their time to practice.

He laid down three conditions: (1) that the work in town should never assume proportions which would be inconsistent with my treating the Law School work as being the main thing; (2) that I should omit no lecture on account of the work in town; and (3) that I should postpone in any one year not more than five per cent of my lectures on account of work in town.

I have enjoyed the combination of teaching and practice, and believe it has been good both for me and for the students. Good for me because the necessity of holding my own against seasoned, experienced practising lawyers guarded against too much theorizing and too much self-complacency. Good for the students because it inspires them to harder work if they feel that what they are learning will pretty surely prove to be reliable when they tackle the practice; and nothing interests students more than a talk about the best way to handle a pending, undecided case. I am convinced that the notion that a professor of law should keep aloof from the practice (a notion which is now much in vogue) is all wrong, — at least for the majority of professors.

To review all my cases in practice is out of the question, and I will speak only of some of my earlier ones. It is those early cases, when attracting a new client was a thrilling experience, that I remember best.

I have said above (page 4) that in the college days I not infrequently was in the library at Shady Hill of Professor Charles Eliot Norton. It never occurred to me that my relations with him would ever be of any financial advantage to me. But fifteen years later, they were. It came about in this wise:

In 1907, Ellery Sedgwick was fired with an ambition to acquire control of the *Atlantic Monthly* and to edit it. He was Harvard '94, in a class ahead of me, and I had known him, but not well. Among those whom he consulted about the *Monthly* project was Professor Norton, and Professor Norton suggested to him that he should consult me about the legal end.

I well remember passing a pleasant and most interesting evening with him at the St. Botolph (the first Boston club to which I was elected). We discussed the matter from both the financial and the legal ends. Thereafter, he opened negotiations with Mr. George H. Mifflin, then the head of Houghton Mifflin Company. Mr. Mifflin did not drop dead at the thought of selling the *Monthly*. But it had had a distinguished past, and Mr. Mifflin regarded himself and his associates as trustees for the discriminating reading public of something precious. He wanted assurances that the *Monthly* in new hands would be conducted in such a manner that there would be no lowering of standards. Mr. Sedgwick was as keen as Mr. Mifflin that there should be no lowering of standards, — he was out to improve, not deteriorate. But he wanted a free hand. He did not want to buy a magazine and then find that the seller had reserved a veto power over what he was to do.

They came to an impasse, and at Mr. Sedgwick's request I went with him to confer with Mr. Mifflin. I asked Mr. Mifflin to state as specifically as he could what were the standards he wished should surely be maintained. He did so. I asked Mr. Sedgwick if he took exception to any of these standards. 'Not at all,' he said, 'but as the years go on, some specific points may arise where Mr. Mifflin and I might disagree as to whether they were in conformity to those standards. If that happens, I want my decision, after Mr. Mifflin and I have talked it out, to be decisive.' Mr. Mifflin was not willing to consent to that.

Finally I suggested to them (1) that the contract of sale and purchase should contain a covenant that the magazine should be conducted according to the standards Mr. Mifflin had outlined; (2) that part of the purchase price should be paid in shares of a purchasing corporation, such shares to represent a substantial, but minority, interest; (3) that if any difference should arise as to whether proposed acts were in conformity to the standards, the matter should be submitted to arbitration; (4) that if the decision of the arbitrators was in favor of Mr. Sedgwick, Mr. Mifflin should acquiesce; (5) but that if their decision was in favor of

Mr. Mifflin, Mr. Sedgwick should have the option either of acquiescing or of buying out the minority shares at a valuation for cash.

They both accepted that at once, and the sun burst through the clouds. In due time the necessary corporation (the Atlantic Monthly Company) was formed and the transaction was completed along those lines.

I digress to point out how one thing leads to another in building up a practice. Not long afterward, serious labor troubles broke out at The Riverside Press, and Mr. Mifflin asked me to be his counsel. I relished Mr. Mifflin. He was a hard fighter, but he never hit below the belt. The labor troubles were not easily adjusted, but in due time they were adjusted on certain broad lines which both employer and employee found acceptable. And the labor policy then inaugurated laid a foundation upon which were built many years of relations between employer and employed which were profitable to both.

And not long after the *Monthly* episode, I was asked to act as New England counsel for the Authors' League of America. I suppose (but do not know) that the fact that I had acted as counsel for the Atlantic Monthly Company was at least one of the things that led to that.

As such counsel, I met a number of interesting people who needed help and appreciated it when given. Among those was Mrs. Eleanor H. Porter. She had written a story about Pollyanna, and had submitted it for publication to a religious paper (I think the name was the *Christian Herald*). They paid her one hundred dollars for the serial rights, with which sum she was well content. A publishing house saw the possibilities of the story as a book and offered to publish it for her. She gladly signed the contract presented.

The book had an immense sale, — several hundred thousands (I dare say that the sales including reprints even went into seven figures). Of course Mrs. Porter proceeded to write another book and submitted it to her publishers. Of course they were glad to have it. But, when it came to the question of terms, the publishers took the position that, under the contract she had signed, Mrs. Porter had agreed that the publishers were entitled to publish all other books she might ever write *on the same terms*. That jolted her, and she came to me.

The royalty under the contract was low, — the lowest I have ever seen. But, when that contract was made, Mrs. Porter was

an unknown, or at least obscure, author, and I incline to think
that on all the facts Mrs. Porter had no ground for complaint in
law or equity, *if* that clause about the future had not been inserted. I told Mrs. Porter that it was a matter fit to lay before a
court of equity and that I thought that there was more than a
fighting chance that equity would strike down the clause. I also
advised her to say to her publishers that they might publish the
new book, not on the old terms, but on such terms as would be
given by other reputable publishers, — in a word, that they might
have the first chance to publish at market rates. And then I
went to Houghton Mifflin Company and asked them to state
specifically what royalty they would be prepared to pay, if Mrs.
Porter were legally free to deal with them; and they did so.

Then I took the position with the publishers that they could
have the book at these terms, but that, if they declined to give
such terms, she proposed to publish it through another publishing
house. I warned her that she would be facing litigation, — that
in all probability her publishers would seek to enjoin her. 'Shall
I be arrested?' 'Well, it will not be quite so bad as that, but an
officer of the law will no doubt pay you a call and leave a paper
with you, and he may be a little gruff.'

Of course what I was after was to put the publishers in a position where they would have to establish that equity should prevent what they would say was a threatened breach of contract.
Even if the act would be in law a breach of contract, I felt pretty
sure (although I was not cocky about it) that a court of equity
would regard this clause as so hard that, for the sake of protect-
ing both Mrs. Porter and other unknown authors in like situation, it would decline to give equitable relief.

The parties eventually compromised, which was the sensible
thing for both. The publishers got the second book, at a somewhat increased royalty, but the old contract was cancelled. Then
I advised Mrs. Porter to make contracts with Houghton Mifflin
Company on the basis of the figures they had given from time
to time (so long as the relations continued satisfactory).

They published several books written by her, and the relations
between them and her were profitable to both. She was poor
when she came to me, but, when her untimely death came not so
many years after and her husband asked me to settle her estate,
I found that the estate was worth about a third of a million.

If I revealed what I charged her for my services in this matter,
there are not a few lawyers who would laugh at me as a piker.

But I have never had an itch for a great fortune. Enough is as good as a feast (and better for the spiritual digestion).

In 1921, the finances of Harvard University were in such a condition that it seemed wise to appoint a University committee to consider them. I was made a member of that committee, and the chairman of a sub-committee to make recommendations for increases in tuition in various departments of the University. That brought me into pleasant, profitable relations with Mr. Charles Francis Adams, who was then the Harvard Treasurer. At first the six members of the sub-committee had no less than four differing views, but we kept at it until we were able unanimously to make certain recommendations which were, in turn, unanimously adopted by each department affected. That report is on file in the Harvard Archives, and contains some interesting figures which I think may be consulted even today with profit.

In 1921–22, Dean Pound took a sabbatical, and both President Lowell and he asked me to serve as Acting Dean. I complied, but with regret, for it necessarily meant abstention from all practice for the year. That was a very busy, and in some ways a very trying, year.

In the summer of 1927, I resigned, the resignation to be effective February 1, 1929. For five years I lived abroad, spending about half the year in England, and the other half in Italy. During those five years I did very little legal work, although I gave some lectures in about half a dozen English or Scottish Universities.

It was a mistake for me to retire at the age of fifty-six. I had led a very active life, and soon began to long for the smell of legal gunpowder. In 1934, I again became a member of the Harvard Law Faculty. I shall be seventy next January, and my latest (and last) resignation is to take effect February 1, 1943.

During the nine years my work has been, and will be, confined to Property I. As I am convinced that so far as the training of students is concerned (which training should always be given the centre of the stage), the first-year courses are the most important courses in the School, I have cheerfully served, but I confess that there have been moments when into my mind have crept nostalgic thoughts about that old course in Corporations.

Travel and the reading of books other than legal books have
played a large part in moulding my mind.

I have travelled in over a dozen countries and have taken
walking-trips in eight of them. Travelling according to Baedeker
and following the man from Cook's yields little of cultural value
(although no doubt it does help in keeping up with the Joneses).
Find something worth while, — some beauty of nature, some
artistic triumph of man, some interesting customs of a people.
Having found it, linger over it.

I have no desire ever to see again Berlin or Rome or Paris or
London. But, when the great bell of Time shall peal forth a
happier hour, it would give me much pleasure to find myself some
years hence once more in Florence. If there is any combination
more soothing and satisfying than the Duomo, the Ponte Vec-
chio, the Pitti, the Uffizzi, and Fiesole, I have not found it.

I have always been, and still am, an omnivorous reader. I said
above that it is not easy for me to make *intimate* friendships with
other human beings. But many books are my intimate friends.
In times of exasperation or trouble they have never failed to give
me solace. And they have done much to mould my literary style
and to mould my philosophy of life. My most intimate friends
are the Bible, the *Meditations* of Marcus Aurelius, Shakespeare,
the *Letters* of Dorothy Osborne, *Silas Marner*, *Cranford*, and
Sense and Sensibility.

Scarcely any of the young men of today are familiar with
Marcus Aurelius. There is much that is admirable in the philosophy of life of that old Roman. I have therefore collected some
passages from his little book and arranged them in an order of
my own, and will close this chapter by setting forth such passages in such order, in the hope that at least some young men will
read these passages and ponder over them:

> Think of the sum of being, and in what a morsel of it you
> partake; the sum of time, compared with the brief atom assigned
> to you; of destiny, and the jot you are of it.

> Men have reason; therefore, in your dealings with them own
> the social tie. Men exist for each other. Teach them, then, or
> bear with them. Practise attention to what others say and do
> your best to get into the speaker's mind.

> At what hour you will you can retire into yourself. Dig within.
> Within is the fountain of good; ever dig and it will ever well
> forth water. Try to persuade men, but act, whether it is liked
> or not, when principles of justice so demand.

About learning, no parade. Have at command thoughts brief and elemental. Let no man have it in his power to say of truth that you lack simplicity. No star wears a veil.

Have the cheer that comes of doing a few things, and doing them well. Stick only to the work in hand and to the tool you have for doing it. Rise to the occasion always with a smile. No one tires of service rendered.

Habituate yourself to the perception of all-pervading change; dwell upon it continually, and order your thoughts according.

Let not the future disturb you. You will face it, if so be, with the same reason which is yours to meet the present.

You embark, you make life's journey, you come to port, you step out. Serenely greet the journey's end.

Chapter Two

EFFECTIVE TEACHING METHODS

THIS chapter is intended to be helpful to relatively young men (say, those who are still on the sunny side of forty), and particularly to those who offer a first-year course in a law school. The desirable methods of teaching a second-year or a third-year course differ from the desirable methods of teaching a first-year course, but much of what I say below is applicable to all teaching of law. I make the following points:

1. The giving of a substantial amount of reliable information and the training of the minds of the students are *both* important. But the instructor should lay about twice as much emphasis upon training as upon information.

2. If a choice had to be made between an exclusive use of the case method or an exclusive use of the lecture method, the case method should be used. But I see no reason why either method should be exclusively used. Do not make a fetish of the case method. So far as giving information is concerned, a considerable use of the lecture method is desirable. Two examples of the lecture method are given at pages 62–78.

3. The main thing is the training of students so that they may be enabled to become *accurate*, *clear*, and *terse* in their statement of facts and issues, and *sensible* in their exercise of judgment. It is wise not to try to do more for first-year students than to help them to be accurate, clear, terse, and sensible.

4. The first thing is to guide them in the making of abstracts. A student should first read a case rather rapidly so as to see what it is all about. Then he must determine with care *just what was the question which the court was called upon to decide.*

Most of the cases are cases in an appellate court, and the higher court will be considering the propriety of the actions of the trial judge. Did the trial judge err in receiving or rejecting certain testimony? Did he err in leaving the case to the jury or in directing a verdict? Did he err in his charge to the jury? This inventory of questions is not exhaustive, but it covers the ground in the bulk of cases.

Having reached his conclusion, the student should write that question or questions, accurately, clearly, tersely. This is the first part of the abstract.

Then he should write an accurate, clear, terse statement of so many of the facts and of so much of the pleadings as are pertinent to this question, *discarding all else*. Many students when they begin to write abstracts really do not do much more than to copy large portions of the report. This is all wrong. The pertinent facts and the pertinent pleadings can, with brains, usually be reduced to a few lines, and that reducing, eliminating process is very helpful in training the mind. This is the second part of an abstract.

Then the student should write what was the decision of the court. This can usually be done in a single word, or, at most, a single line. This is the third part of the abstract.

Then the student should write, accurately, clearly, tersely, what were the *reasons* given by the court for its result. Sometimes there is only a single reason given. But not infrequently the court will give alternative reasons. And not infrequently the court will drop a dictum or dicta (a dictum is something which a court sees fit to say as to the proper answer to a question which is *not* presented on the facts and pleadings in the case). Dicta are obviously of not so much weight as a reason or an alternative reason, but unquestionably they are given some weight and have played a substantial part in the development of the law.

Distinguish, therefore, between (*a*) a sole reason; (*b*) alternative reasons; (*c*) dicta. This is the fourth, and final, part of the abstract.

The ability to make a good abstract can come only after long practice. The dead-in-earnest student will usually find that in the first few months he will scrap his first draft, and write a second, and sometimes a third or fourth draft before he has achieved something which seems to him to be accurate, clear, and terse.

A student should make his abstracts in solitude, relying only upon himself. And even after he has made them, he should not compare them with those of any fellow student, — if he does look forward to a checking by comparing with others, it will weaken his sense of the necessity of doing the work *wholly* on his own.

There is one thing about abstracts which is so important that it will be made the subject of a separate point.

5. Encourage students to use the A, B, C technique. For example: In every pledge case let A stand for the pledgor; let B stand for the pledgee; let C stand for the assignee of the debt and security, if both are assigned to one person; and let C stand for the assignee of the debt and D for the assignee of the security, if the debt and security are assigned to different persons. This makes for terseness. It avoids discussion in class as to who was who. And — much more important — *it facilitates the comparison of one case with another.*

In *Margin Customers* (at pages 246–47), one of my seventeen adverse criticisms of Judge Cardozo's opinion in *Wood* v. *Fisk* is the fact that he cited the case of *Donald* v. *Suckling* as though it were pertinent to the case at bar. But in *Donald* v. *Suckling* the contest was between A and *C*, while in *Wood* v. *Fisk* it was between A and *B*. If Judge Cardozo had analyzed the two cases in the terms of the A, B, C technique, it is hardly thinkable that he would have cited a case as an authority for a proposition which was not before the court and upon which not one of the four judges even dropped a dictum.

Students do not see the value of the A, B, C technique at first. They are inclined to think that it is a fussy requirement, — much ado about nothing. Keep at them until they do see the value of it. If they are fit to be lawyers, they will eventually see it and will come to value it highly and to use it instinctively.

6. By far the most difficult part of teaching is to conduct, *in an effective manner*, the classroom discussions. Merely to lecture is pretty easy; the instructor gets the points in orderly arrangement in his mind, takes the platform, and just tells the students what is what. *Some* straight lecturing is, I not only concede but urge, both permissible and desirable (see pages 62–78); *but* be on your guard against doing too much of it. You will be tempted to do a lot of it, not only because it is the easiest way, but also because the students lap it up. My experience leads me to believe that a large proportion of the students, on coming to a law school fresh from the *dolce far niente* college years, would rather walk two miles than think for three minutes. If the instructor will only give them something that they can write down and

memorize, the students will rise up and call him blessed. But too much lecturing is bad for them, — very bad.

Put classroom discussions in the centre of the stage. The discussions cannot be cut-and-dried (as lectures may). To carry on discussions effectively two things are requisite:

(1) The instructor must be a full man, — he must really have himself mastered the topic to be discussed so that he is quite clear as to what he thinks (at present), as to why he thinks it, and as to what the *present* state of the authorities is. In a word, he must know his business.

(2) The instructor must *also* be a ready man. He must be able to catch as catch can. He must be able to adjust himself, and quickly to adjust himself, to *any*thing that a student may say, — developing the good, demolishing the bad. Some instructors who are sound lawyers seem to be unable to acquire the suppleness and adroitness of mind which will enable them to carry on *stimulating* classroom discussions.

But if a young instructor has the ambition to be at the top of the teaching profession, he *must* be both a full man and a *ready* man. There is plenty of room at the top.

7. There are two points about classroom discussions which have given me much anxious thought, and about which I wish to write at some length, devoting a separate point to each.

When I joined the Harvard Law Faculty, my thought, often expressed, was that any student might ask any question at any time. I was (and am) strong for the ideal of freedom of thought and speech, and to give all students such unlimited opportunities seemed to me to be the right way to implement that ideal, as applied to classroom discussions.

But experience has convinced me that that just does not work. I deeply regret that, but 'tis so. The trouble is that an aggressive few speak again and again. There are many loquacious students who are really not much good. They thoroughly enjoy taking the floor, but the other students get bored, — the class goes dead. Nothing is so deadly to a class as a lot of cat-talk. Moreover, the very fact that some men do thus bore their mates by loose and excessive talking has a strong tendency to make talking unfashionable. The result is that many good men hesitate to speak lest they be classified as among the mouth-organs. The loquacious are usually (not always) weak; the strong are usually (not always) silent.

This is serious. After long pondering over the problem thus

presented, I adopted, and in recent years have enforced, two regulations:

(1) No student shall speak unless he is called upon by name.

(2) No student shall raise his hand seeking opportunity to speak unless I call for volunteers (as I not infrequently do).

I go around the class so that in the course of the year each student shall have, approximately at least, as much chance to participate in the discussion as any other student, and I guard the talking student or students (for the oftener that two students with opposing views can be pitted against each other, the better) from any interruption whatever from other students.

There is reason in all things, and I believe that these two regulations make a reasonable limitation on freedom of speech. A few students kick against those regulations; they tell me that they never were subjected to anything like that in the good old college days (and it may well be that that is true); and they even object to such regulations as contrary both to the Declaration of Independence and to the Fourteenth Amendment to the Constitution of the United States. Sometimes the disregard by a particular student of such regulations is so persistent that it is necessary for me to write him a letter, setting forth why I think those regulations are desirable, and appealing to him to cooperate. But very few students give me any trouble; true it is that exasperators are a hardy annual, but during the year now drawing to a close I have had to write to only three. The great bulk of the students see the value in these regulations and cordially comply and cooperate.

I am clear that these regulations are for the good of a class, *considered as a whole*. If there are a few students who are troublesome, do not let that even dent your serenity; remember that no man can make an omelette without breaking a few eggshells.

8. The second point with regard to the classroom discussions is the use of the 'Yes' or 'No' technique. Answer the question put to you, — 'Yes' or 'No.'

Is that fair? Well, it depends on the question put whether a 'Yes' or 'No' answer may fairly be expected. There are many, many questions to which such an answer cannot fairly be expected. Probably most of the readers have heard of the lawyer who on cross-examining a witness asked him: 'Have you stopped beating your wife?'

An *indispensable* condition to the use of the 'Yes' or 'No' technique is that the instructor should be able to frame, and should frame, his question so that a 'Yes' or 'No' answer may fairly be expected. But there are many, many such questions.

What I have the greatest difficulty in making the student realize is that the 'Yes' or 'No' answer does not *close* the discussion. It simply opens it. Further questions will surely follow. *In due time* he will be given opportunity to express all that is in his mind (if it is in coherent shape).

The 'Yes' or 'No' technique is a step-by-step technique. That's the point. Don't miss that. For example: There is a famous Pennsylvania case entitled *Rerick* v. *Kern* (14 S. & R. 267). A and B owned adjoining pieces of land; a stream flowed into A's land, then divided on A's land, and flowed onto B's land in two branches. B was minded to build a mill on his land, and he wanted to do acts on A's land which would prevent the division of the stream so that he might at his mill, when built, have the benefit of the waterpower of the whole stream. B asked A for permission to do such acts on A's land as would prevent the division of the stream. A said he had no objection. Thereupon B did those acts, and thereafter built his mill. Some time later A undid what B had done on A's land, so that thereafter the water flowed as it had been accustomed to flow before B had done these acts.

Now, what B obviously wanted was a right to have the water come to his land in one stream *indefinitely*. If he had such right, B would have an easement in A's land. The law is that an easement may be created only (1) by a writing under seal showing the intent to give such right, or (2) by adverse user. Even if an *oral* contract has been made for an easement, an obstacle to the specific enforcement of that contract is presented by the Statute of Frauds which provides that no interest in land may be created without a writing.

I consider that all of the questions listed below are questions to which a 'Yes' or 'No' answer may fairly be expected:

(1) Had there been any such lapse of time that there is any possibility that an easement had been acquired by adverse user?

(2) Was there any instrument in writing under seal creating such easement?

(3) Was there a contract for such an easement between A and B?

(4) Assuming that there was a contract, was there on the

facts anything to take the case out of the Statute of Frauds?

(5) Had B tried to get something for nothing?

If a student will face these five questions and answer each of them 'Yes' or 'No,' he gradually clarifies the problem and narrows the issue. And at long last the question can be faced: Was there *anything* on these facts that should give B a right to complain of A? That is a very difficult question and courts have differed, and still differ, as to what the answer should be. But if a student assumes to answer that question without the preliminary, winnowing, 'Yes or No' method, he will go round and round in ever-widening circles.

No lawyer can be an efficient cross-examiner unless he is master of the 'Yes' and 'No' technique. (Do not forget that one part of this is to be able to put questions to which such an answer may fairly be expected.) And I am convinced that no jurist on or off the bench can be an efficient jurist unless he is accustomed in his thinking to put 'Yes' or 'No' questions to himself, and to require himself to give an answer to himself in that form.

9. There is another problem, distinguishable from problems as to classroom discussions, but closely related to such problems.

The ideal lecture closes at a point where the students are in a turmoil of thoughts. Some of them, many of them, rush for the desk. They want the instructor right then and there to put them out of mental distress, to clear it all up, and put their minds at peace.

It is a mistake to do that for them. Let them go away, unsatisfied. Make them realize that they must do some mighty hard thinking *themselves* both by discussions with their fellow students out of class and ultimately by pondering in solitude.

But balance this by encouraging them, *after* they have discussed the matter with fellow students and have pondered over these things in their hearts, to reduce to writing (in accurate, clear, terse form) any question or questions which are still bothering them and hand those questions in. Collect the questions, arrange them in some order, and then hold, at rather frequent intervals, a question hour (which will often develop into a double-header) in which those questions are read, and the instructor gives his answers.

My experience is that that works, and works splendidly. The methods stated in points 6 to 9, both inclusive, have fourfold advantages: (1) they give to everyone his fair share of the instructor's time and attention; (2) they drive it home to the students that they *must* train their minds by helping themselves (the most important point of all); (3) there is something going on all the time which is of interest to the whole class; and (4) in due time the students receive the benefit of the instructor's own thoughts. Be clear, but do not be clear *too soon*.

10. *But* balance all that has been said above by insisting upon, and giving the fullest recognition to, the highly important fact that, after all has been done which can properly be done to clarify and narrow issues, there will frequently be questions, and perhaps many questions, on which intelligent men may well differ. Encourage the students to reach their own conclusions. Encourage them to disagree with you. Encourage them to think and let think. An instinct to think and let think, coupled with an intellectual conscience, is the supreme good.

11. Do not tell the students more than ten per cent of what you know about the subject matter of the course; and know so much that ten per cent of what you know will be as much as they can be expected to assimilate in their first year.

12. Keep a record of how the men have acquitted themselves in the classroom, and if an examination paper is on the doubtful line, re-read it with benevolent assumptions in favor of (but only in favor of) men with a pretty good classroom record.

13. Encourage them to regard discussions among themselves out of class as very important, — hardly less important than the discussions in class. A group of four is, usually, an ideal discussion group as to size.

14. Encourage them to give as high as a quarter of their time in the first year to participate in moot-cases (the Ames Competition at Harvard and similar competitions elsewhere).

15. Do not talk to the students as from the mount. Keep your eye on the receiving end. Aim at the low C men. Are you enabling others to see what you see? On the one hand never be cheap; never make a joke or coin an epigram for the sake of raising a laugh; let the jokes or the epigrams or the homely illustrations be spontaneous, — generated by something that a student has said. But, on the other hand, do not feel that it is *infra dig.* for you to use an apt, spontaneously generated, joke or epigram or homely illustration. That will often get the thought over when everything else has gone off the student's mind like water off a duck's back.

16. Do not get into a legal rut. Have some wholesome inter-

ests outside of the law. Law is only a small part of life, and it is impossible to achieve a proper philosophy of the law unless one has a proper philosophy of life.

17. Try to make the students realize that a satisfying lifetime at the bar usually requires *four* things: (1) a sound body; (2) a pleasing personality; (3) a good intellect; (4) a character that inspires confidence.

There are a good many young men who are unduly aggressive and are much more conscious of what is due *to* them from others than of what is due *from* them to others. Others avoid such men, — they just do not see them (if they see them first). Manners have a lot to do with attracting, and retaining, associates and clients.

Character has even more to do with attracting and retaining associates and clients. I know no asset that any man can have which will contribute so much to a legitimate and enduring success at the bar as the confidence of other people that he can be trusted always to do the decent thing.

Health, manners, brains, character — it usually takes all four to have a permanent satisfying success at the bar. Don't let the students get brains too close to the camera. Brains are cheap in the marketplace. It takes brains to be a success at the bar, but brains alone will not get a man very far.

Chapter Three

EFFECTIVE JURISTIC STYLE

THE literary style, or lack of literary style, of many judges, professors of law, and editors of, and contributors to, law reviews is deplorable (or, at least, it so seems to me). What is the trouble? Three sources of trouble may be mentioned: (1) sloppy thinking; (2) a love for 'half-tones'; (3) a love for resounding words and expressions.

1. *Sloppy thinking.* There is a very close connection between sloppy thinking and sloppy writing. If the writer has not wrestled with the angel until his thoughts are clear in his own mind, how can he possibly write something which will be clear to the minds of others? An effective literary style is achieved only by an infinite capacity for taking pains.

The prevalent habit of dictating thoughts rather than writing them in longhand has done much, very much, to lower the general average of literary style. I am not in favor of the abolition of stenographers; no doubt dictation is an important time-saver with respect to routine matters, chatty letters, and the like. But woe to the jurist who dictates. Possibly some extraordinary men are safe in dictating on any subject; one marvels at the reputed (and probably actual) capacity of Julius Caesar in that respect. But there is at most only a tiny fraction of jurists who can safely dictate when they wish to express themselves on legal matters of any difficulty.

Sharpen the good old pencil. *Write* out your thoughts. The very fact that that is slower is all to the good, — your mind has a much better chance to keep up with your hand than with your tongue. The very fact that it is laborious is also all to the good, — it inclines you to brevity, and to the use of shorter words.

2. *A love for 'half-tones.'* 'Half-tones' are usually 'half-truths.' Distinguish sharply between (*a*) saying something which is half true and half false, and (*b*) an orderly marshalling

of opposing considerations, each of which is entitled to *some* weight.

3. *A love for resounding words and expressions.* There are many persons who have that love. Once upon a time a clergyman was seeking to give comfort to a dying parishioner. 'You have found great comfort,' said he, 'in your Bible, have you not?' 'Yes, yes,' the dying old lady said. 'And what has been the word in the Bible that has been to you the source of the greatest comfort?' 'Mesopotamia,' answered the old lady. A word of six syllables. So far as I know, there is no word in the Bible of more than five syllables, except the names of persons or places, and there is only a small fraction of more than three. For example: In the fifty-first Psalm about seventy-four per cent of the words are words of one syllable, over ninety per cent are words of one or two syllables, and about ninety-eight per cent are words of one, two, or three syllables. Yet the old lady treasured most a word of six syllables, which was devoid of any spiritual light or leading.

Orators like Cicero and writers like Gibbon have rejoiced in resounding words and expressions. I am sorry to say that the list of other orators and writers who have relished the like is a very long list. And the use of such words and expressions no doubt does impress persons of a certain (or uncertain) grade of intelligence. The use of such words and expressions has done much to cause a revulsion against 'oratory.' I have always found that most jurymen like to have counsel express themselves in simple, homely words and expressions. That is wholesome.

Stop trying to impress people by the use of long words, or words with which the ordinary man is unfamiliar. I have read somewhere (although I cannot at the moment lay my hand on the quotation) a statement by an eminent jurist that it was not fitting that rules of law should be expressed in terms which those who are unlearned in the law could comprehend. Woe to such jurists.

There is nothing else that I have written that I so much desire should have a wide, enduring influence as the first two pages in the preface to the treatise on *Margin Customers*, which were as follows:

> *Style:* I note with deep and increasing regret that some jurists on the bench and many jurists off the bench evidence no instinct for simplicity and terseness of expression. They clothe their thoughts with a prodigality of drapery which ought to be as repulsive to the wholesome-minded as the rich plush which some

decades ago was regarded as *le dernier cri* in the very best railroad, steamship, and hotel circles.

Some of these jurists must have been born with a long spoon in the mouth. They make four words grow where only one word grew before, and rejoice that it has been given to them to add to the national wealth. Some of them even invent new nomenclatures, juristic Mumbo Jumbo, words which are unintelligible, without explanation, to intelligent laymen. They build themselves stilts and thump about making loud noises, and are exceeding glad that they have grown to giant size, and ever and anon duck a low star.

How to correct this? If a student asks my advice, I say to him:

1. Never dictate anything which calls for careful thinking. Write out everything (except quotations) in longhand. If you dictate, you are likely to get into a habit of using words of many syllables like 'formulated' or 'constituted.' If you write in longhand you are likely to get into a habit of using words of one syllable like 'made' or 'was.'

2. Make it a habit of life to spend ten minutes a day in reading something in the Psalms or Proverbs or Gospels; and treasure the short, terse, depicting, dynamic, devastating words and expressions.

3. See to it that not less than sixty-six per cent of your words are words of one syllable, and that not less than eighty-three per cent are words of one or two syllables.

4. Go over the drafts as they come back from the typist and rub and rub and rub again until you have massaged away every muddy word and every waste word.

5. If you are dealing with a tough juristic topic, lighten the strain from time to time. If one page has to contain a headache, balance it with another page that contains a smile. A joke may be the most effective of arguments, and the most dignified dignity is an unstilted dignity.

6. *But* avoid being 'cheap' as you would shun the plague. You are living in a picture age; picturesqueness is the order of the day. All right, adapt yourself, be picturesque; but *never* be cheap. And be keenly conscious of the fact that the line between the picturesque and the cheap is *not* a bright line.

7. Let learning be your servant, not your master; the deepest learning is the learning that conceals learning. The bread of an idea is worth more than a stone of information. Do not spread out in full your laboratory notes. Do not be *magis in operatione quam in opere.* Appraise your 'productivity,' not by quantity, but by quality. Read much, discuss much, ponder most, write a little.

Chapter Four

IN THE NEWSPAPERS

JAMES BARR AMES
THE APPRECIATION OF A STUDENT AND COLLEAGUE
Boston Transcript, January 15, 1910

DEAN AMES made students think. He loved to teach, and he was a masterly teacher. He would bring out an idea, and the idea would seem entirely reasonable. He would bring out another idea, and that, too, would seem entirely reasonable. Gradually it would dawn on the student that the two ideas were quite inconsistent, and that he must decide which was right. The student was interested, stimulated, tantalized. The lectures by the Dean, especially in the course on Trusts, caused great mental disturbance, not to say anguish. He baptized men in brain fire.

The members of the Faculty of the Harvard Law School believe that the most helpful way to teach law is to discuss with the students specific cases that have been decided by the courts. How does the judicial mind work? What considerations influence judges? Given a definite state of facts, how would the judges probably decide? The sum of legal knowledge is now immense. The stock of information that can be given to students is relatively small. The School does not attempt to store the minds of the students with answers to every legal question; it attempts to train their minds so that they may know how to go about it to get the answer to any legal question.

This is teaching by the case system. The introduction of this method was due to Professor Langdell, who preceded Professor Ames as Dean of the School. Dean Ames was the disciple of Langdell. Langdell originated, Ames spread, the idea.

He spread it in two ways. Each year scores (and lately hundreds) of young men were leaving the School who had been stimulated and strengthened intellectually by him. They prized the training, and they found that it told in actual practice. In the second place, as other law schools wished to adopt the method, he gladly helped to make its introduction easy. Harvard has never made any attempt to guard the case system as a trade secret; it has, on the contrary, with both hands done its utmost to help other institutions to adopt it. Dean Ames was foremost in this. He put himself at the service of every law teacher in the country who wanted light and leading.

It is not too much to say that today, considering the country as a whole, the case system is the dominant method used in teaching law. No one — not excepting Langdell himself — has contributed more to this result than Ames. His influence has been national.

He analyzed the cases with his students by the Socratic method. He questioned much; he answered little. Those who came to hear the law laid down went away to ponder what it ought to be. He loved the battle of wits, but he never argued simply for the sake of victory. He helped men in many ways, but most of all because he made them help themselves.

He never practised at the bar, and was a legal philosopher rather than a lawyer. In some ways this marred his efficiency, but in other ways it increased it. He took broad views which could be taken only from heights to which few, if any, practitioners could ever rise. He viewed the law as a whole, and he searched for the great principles that underlay it. In constructive legal imagination, he has probably never been equalled by any person learned in the common law. He had the most suggestive mind with which I have ever come in contact.

He loved to evolve and apply a legal principle. Once satisfied that a certain principle was sound, he would look for applications of it in all branches of the law, and his enthusiasm would lead him to believe that judges had acted on the principle in deciding certain cases where (in all probability) the judges had been profoundly unconscious of any such principle. This tendency grew on him in later years. It made him warp the authorities, and it led him into inaccurate statements as to the state of the authorities. I think this was his greatest fault, but it was hardly to be expected that a mind could be so original and constructive without this fault. He did not state the authorities — he illuminated them.

He would defend his legal principles as though they were his young. In the case of *Price* v. *Neal*, A was the holder of a draft upon which the signature of the drawer had been forged. B, the drawee, paid the draft. At the time of the payment both A and B believed the draft to be genuine. When the forgery was discovered, B sought to recover back from A the money paid, but the court held that he could not. The Dean believed that this case was simply an illustration of a very broad principle, — that if both men acted in good faith, equity would let the loss lie where it fell. I differed — not believing that there was any such general principle running through the law, or that there ought to be. 'If you yourself should, in the best of faith, take my money for some worthless thing,' I said to him, 'I have entire confidence that, forthwith upon your discovering it was worthless, you would insist upon reimbursing me.' The Dean grew almost indignant. 'I would do no such thing,' he said. 'I would not pay you a penny.' I might think ill of him, but I must not think he would deviate from the true principle of *Price* v. *Neal*.

Legal history had great attractions for him. Within the four corners of a Year Book, he was in Paradise. Less than a year ago he said: 'If I did just what I wanted to do, I would give myself up to legal history.' He has written a few articles on legal history which will always endure. It is a great pity that he did not write more.

His personality was one of great charm. He was sincerely interested in the welfare of every student. He was invariably courteous, and altogether the gentleman. He had a patience that was stupidity-proof. He gave himself lavishly to any student who wanted to talk to him at any time on any subject to any length. He swayed the hearts, as well as the minds, of his students. There are thousands of men today whose grief is real because Ames is dead.

He was thoughtful in a way that a man is seldom thoughtful toward other men. During my first year in the Faculty, I lectured, among other things, on Equity Jurisprudence. It was a difficult year. Again and again I sought out the Dean to talk with him about points in equity that were troubling me. It was not only that he talked freely and very suggestively, but after the talks were over — sometimes days and even weeks after they were over — I would find on my desk some volume of the Reports, with a little slip of paper directing my attention to a particular authority and a few scribbled words in the Dean's hand indicating how, to his mind, this authority bore on the point we had talked about.

During the six years that I was his junior colleague I cannot remember any important question of policy affecting the School on which I did not vote *contrary* to the Dean. I am sure that this made not the slightest difference in his kindly feeling toward me.

With all his gentleness, he was a firm man. He was considerate, not afraid. When a student in Harvard College, he was captain of the nine. In 1894–95 he was chairman of the Athletic Committee, and when he came to believe that Harvard's athletic relations with Yale ought not to continue, he did not hesitate in taking his part in severing all such relations for a period of years.

He discharged his duties as dean with great conscientiousness, and gave personal attention to the details. He did not know how to delegate work, and he made no use of modern business methods. I do not believe that he ever dictated anything to a stenographer. He administered the loan fund (a fund to supply loans to students to be repaid by them after they had established themselves), and he did not even buy a book of blank promissory notes, — the bodies of all the notes are written out in his own hand.

So long as he was sure he was not infringing upon the rights of others, he was oblivious to their comments. He utterly lacked self-consciousness, and he would go at a dog-trot through the streets of Cambridge, or even Boston, without its ever occurring to him that he might be making people stare.

He was not a poor man, but he lived in a very simple house in Cambridge. In summer he went to Castine, Maine, where he had acquired a large tract of land. He liked to be out-of-doors, and to work with his hands.

His living was plain and his thinking was high.

His wife gave into his life the spirit of old-fashioned roses.

Each Tuesday the members of the Law School Faculty lunch together. A few weeks ago, just as the lunch was finishing, the Dean leaned forward in his chair and said: ' I am very sorry to say that I must leave the Law School. It may be only for a short time — till June or next year — or I may not be able to come back at all. I have been examined by three physicians, and none of them can tell me what is the matter with me. But I find I can't remember names. I can't recall the name of any one of you here without extraordinary effort. It has taken me three hours to prepare a lecture that I've usually prepared in half an hour. I must go away at once. Now, I don't want any of you to be unhappy about this. I am not at all unhappy myself. If I never come back, it will not make me unhappy. If this is the end, I shall have had long years of service, and far more in my life than most men ever have. I must leave you to make provision for the School.'

THE STANDARD OIL DECISION

A signed editorial in the *Boston Herald*, May 16, 1911

THE Sherman Anti-Trust Act condemns 'every' combination in restraint of interstate trade and 'every' monopoly of such trade.

In the Northern Securities case, four out of the five judges who formed the majority were of the opinion that this language must be taken literally, and that every combination must be broken, simply because it is a combination, and regardless of the question whether or not the combination is inimical to the public welfare.

The fear that that doctrine would be established as the law by a clear majority of the Court in the Standard Oil case caused the decision to be awaited with such intense interest.

Much more than half of the interstate business in this country is done by business units which are combinations of two or more units, once separate. To resolve back every such larger unit into its elements would produce economic chaos.

Mr. Justice Harlan wrote the opinion in the Northern Securities case, in which this doctrine was laid down, and he still adheres to it. But all the other members of the Court, as now constituted, take the opposite view, and hold that the Act only condemns such combinations as unreasonably restrain trade. The Court says, with frankness, that some general and broad language in previous decisions must henceforth be considered as limited and qualified.

This decision, reached after two arguments, after long deliberation, and by a nearly unanimous Court, may be taken as settling the law. The Sherman Act, by its title, is levelled at only 'unlawful restraints and monopolies,' and the construction which is now placed upon it is well within the bounds of proper judicial interpretation.

The decision against the Standard Oil Company does not necessitate a decision against every business unit which is the result of smaller units. Each larger unit is to be judged according to the circumstances of its own case 'in the light of reason' to determine whether it is against the public welfare.

There is no occasion to fear that this will leave the law hopelessly undefined and confused. In the past the common-law judges have, little by little, defined what contracts in restraint of trade are unreasonable and what are reasonable. It is the strength of the common law that its judges do not try to cover the ground with a single leap, but feel their way step by step. The courts will now, little by little, define what combinations in restraint of trade are unreasonable and what are reasonable. An exercise of judgment by the Court will be necessary in each case, and the Court will be under a duty to make these exercises of judgment, not hastily or capriciously, but slowly and consistently with other judgments, so that the demarcation between the reasonable and the unreasonable will gradually become distinct.

The Sherman Act becomes, not an engine for the wholesale destruction of combinations, but an instrument for compelling the devices of combinations to be used only in a reasonable way.

The decision is likely to be misunderstood, but it is not sweeping or drastic. It establishes the Sherman Act on a rational basis, and that Act ought now to become, not a menace, but a safeguard, to the legitimate economic development of the country.

The review by the Court of the particular facts in the Standard Oil case is a matter of subordinate interest. The Court reviewed the whole history of the business, as well before as after the enactment of the Sherman Act, and noted the means it had employed to strengthen itself, including its control over means of transportation. It was not a development of business by usual methods, but, on the contrary, a course of dealing intended to drive others from the field and to exclude them from their right to trade. And the combination of the various properties into a single ownership (by transfer to the Standard Oil Company of New Jersey) was an act calculated and intended to perpetuate the mastery thus obtained.

PRESIDENT ROOSEVELT'S
SUPREME COURT PLAN

I BELIEVE that it is wise for a member of a law faculty to make a general rule against writing to the press on burning, political questions. My reasons for that are set forth in a statement prepared with care and made at a Faculty meeting (this will be found at pages 50–52). During the thirty and more years that I have been a member of the Harvard Law Faculty I have abstained from such writing with only one exception.

That one exception was made when President Roosevelt announced his Supreme Court Plan. That plan, it seemed to me, was an attack on the independence of the judiciary. And I felt then, and feel now, that every member of the legal profession has a duty to resist such an attack and contribute his bit toward its defeat.

I have long had a profound admiration for Coke, and one of my reasons for that is the manner in which he resisted the attempt of James I to make the courts subservient to his will. When James I was seeking to extend the scope of the royal prerogative, he caused Coke to be sounded. If a certain point came before him, could His Majesty be assured of a decision in favor of prerogative? A copy of Coke's reply (or draft of reply) is still in existence in the library at Holcombe, the residence of one of Coke's descendants. 'If such a question should ever come before me, I will attempt to decide it as in reason and right it ought to be decided.' He was taking no orders. He was giving no assurances. A never-to-be-forgotten answer. (See *Margin Customers*, page 52.)

I was stirred to the depths by President Roosevelt's proposal, and so were many of my colleagues. It seemed to me that not only was it right to speak out on such an occasion, but that it was my duty to speak out, with all my powers.

There was a further fact that was decisive for action. A considerable number of men concerned with legal education came out in favor of the plan. The Yale Law Faculty was for it (and my recollection is that the vote was unanimous or nearly unanimous). William Draper Lewis, once Dean of the University of Pennsylvania Law School, and later at the helm of the American Law Institute, supported it. And James M. Landis, after he had been selected as Dean of the Harvard Law School, but before his

period of service had begun, supported it in a public debate with
Senator Wheeler of Montana which was widely reported in the
press. There was a belief widespread through the nation that
the Harvard Law Faculty also supported the plan; just what
caused that widespread belief is matter of conjecture, but that
there was such widespread belief, I am sure.

This belief was directly contrary to the fact. What the fact
was is shown in a news item carried by the *New York Herald
Tribune* on Monday, March 22, 1937, which was as follows:

Special to the Herald Tribune

CAMBRIDGE, MASS., March 21. — In connection with an open
letter to the United States Senators from Massachusetts, opposing the President's court proposal, made public here today by
Professors Edward H. Warren, Joseph Warren, and Morton C.
Campbell, of the Harvard Law School Faculty, the firstnamed,
Professor Edward H. Warren, was asked if he knew to what extent
the letter represented the views of the Faculty.

His statement follows:

'The common impression is that the bulk of the Harvard Law
School Faculty is in favor of the President's proposal. This is
partly due to the fact that Professor Frankfurter has been a
prominent adviser to the President. It is also partially due to the
fact that Dean-Designate Landis has spoken in favor of the proposal. He did not in so doing assume to state anything but his
personal views, and yet there is an inescapable tendency for the
public to think of him in his capacity as the new Dean and to draw
the conclusion that his views are the views of the Faculty.

'The impression thus created is very much regretted by many
members of the Faculty who feel we are in a false position before
the public. Most of us are very hesitant to talk in public on
questions of burning public interest lest statements made by us as
individuals should be taken as corporate statements. But it is
clear that a false impression has arisen and is widespread in the
minds of the public and that it should be corrected.

'There are thirty men on the Faculty, excluding one who is
on a three years' leave of absence. Of these, nineteen have stated
in public that they are opposed to the proposition. The other
eleven are divided into three groups. First, those who are opposed
to the proposal, but who do not wish to make any public statement of their position; second, those who are non-committal, who
have not reached a final conclusion; third, those who are in favor
of the proposal.

'It is not true that the views of Dean-Designate Landis represent the views of the bulk of the Faculty.'

Letter on Editorial Page

The substance of the open letter from the three Harvard professors is carried as a letter to the editor on the editorial page of the *New York Herald Tribune* today.

What to do about it? I consulted two colleagues, Joseph Warren and Morton Campbell, both of whom had been classmates in the Law School. We discussed the points to be made. When we had agreed on the points, I made a first draft of the proposed letter. There were further consultations and further drafts. The fourth draft was acceptable to all three, and we signed it as our joint statement.

Then we took thought as how best to bring it to the attention of the public. That involved some spade work. We selected a dozen well-known newspapers published in various parts of the country, and I wrote to all, stating that we should like to have it published simultaneously on March 22, and would they be willing to publish it on or after that date with such elements of publicity as seemed to them fitting?

This led to an incident which I have never ceased to relish. The letters mailed, I was one morning at my desk in Langdell Hall, poring over *Coke on Littleton*. Long Distance was on the wire.

Then a voice: 'Is this Professor Warren?'

'Yes.'

'Bull Warren?'

'I have been so called.'

'My name is X. You don't remember me, but I remember you. I took Property I with you in [a year in the early twenties]. I never made a hit with you. You gored me. You tossed me about. At the end of the year you flunked me. I was excluded from the School. I was out on the sidewalk. I had to give up my life desire to be a lawyer and to take a position on this paper. And I've been here ever since. And I've made good, — I'd like you to make a note of that. I've made *very* good, and now I'm at the head of the Publicity Department. What I say as to Publicity almost always goes.

'And now they bring me a letter of yours asking that this paper give publicity to something that you and two of your colleagues have written about the Supreme Court. Ha! *Ha!!* I've been waiting for this for years. I've got you just where I want you.

'And I've only one thing more to say to you, sir, and it's this: If there is anything that you want on this paper, all you've got to do is to ask for it.'

And he hung up, without giving me a chance to say a word.

The letter was published in full or in large part by many newspapers. I cannot now recall all of them, but besides the publication in the *New York Herald Tribune*, on March 22, under the caption 'President-Men,' the *New York Times* published about half a column on March 23, the following day, and the other papers which published the matter in full on March 22 included the *Boston Globe* (in the form of an open letter to the Massachusetts Senators), the *Boston Herald*, the *Boston Post* (with an attention-calling editorial), the *Christian Science Monitor*, the *Baltimore Sun*, the *Atlanta Constitution*, the *Pittsburgh Gazette*, the *Cleveland Plain Dealer*, and the *Chicago News*. And many other newspapers subsequently published the news item in the *New York Herald Tribune* and/or the whole or parts of the letter.

The form in which the letter was published differed slightly in the various papers. The form given below was that which was used by the *Baltimore Sun*:

To the Editor of The Sun — *Sir:*

The President, in advocating his court proposals, justified them by the parable of the three horses used to plow a field, who must 'pull together.' But the legislative, executive, and judiciary branches of this Government are not under a duty to have no differences. If a President vetoes a measure passed by the Congress, he cannot justly be held up to reproach or obloquy as the horse that lay down. On the contrary, it is his duty, under the Constitution, to exercise an independent judgment and, on occasion, to be a check upon the Legislature.

It is also the duty of the judiciary if, exercising an independent judgment, it is convinced that a measure passed by the Legislature violates a provision of the Constitution, so to declare. If it does so declare, it cannot justly be held up to reproach or obloquy as the horse that lay down.

The Constitution protects the rights of the several states, as against the Federal Government, and it protects the rights of minorities, *however small*, on religious questions, on racial questions, on questions involving deprivations of property, or deprivations of the liberty of speech, or deprivations of the right to a fair trial. Whenever the court gives to a state or an individual the protection to which it is convinced that the state or the individual is entitled under the Constitution, it deserves respect, not abuse.

The President's parable reveals a misunderstanding of the nature of our Government. Our Government was designed to be a system of checks and balances. It contemplated an independent Legislature, an independent Executive, and an independent Judiciary. It was designed, consciously and carefully, to guard against a concentration of power in any one branch of the Government.

The framework of our Government may usefully be compared with the framework of the British Government. The British Government has not a system of checks and balances. Power is concentrated in the Legislature, and there are not even two effectively independent branches of the Legislature. The will of the House of Commons is final on some matters at once, and on all other matters after a relatively short period. In substance, the Prime Minister could rule Great Britain as he pleased, *provided* that he had a majority in the House of Commons who were subservient to his will. At present the House of Commons is in the control of independent men, and a Prime Minister would be quickly purged if he had illusions of grandeur. But fill the House of Commons with yes-men, and the substance of British democracy would be gone.

If the President's proposals are enacted by the Senate, we shall have taken a long step away from our system of checks and balances. The President would seem to be in a state of mind where more than the independence of the judiciary is at stake. The independence of the Senate would seem to be threatened, and to be threatened *now*. The President has already great power in his hands — means by which he may attempt to bring the Senate into line. There are apparently Senators who fear that opposition to the President's proposals may cause them to be at a disadvantage in the distribution of patronage, or may cause them to be read out of the Democratic Party, or at least to be deprived of important aid when they come up for renomination.

The President intends to have President-men control the judiciary, and it would appear to be probable that he also intends, if it is necessary in order to accomplish his will, to have President-men control the Senate. If the President relieved Senators from all Presidential pressure, and left each Senator free to exercise his independent judgment on the merits of the proposals, these proposals would, we believe, be rejected decisively.

It will take a good deal of courage by some Senators to exercise an independent judgment. Certain Senators have already shown that they have such courage; but we fear that there will be President-men, creatures whose knees, not their minds, are in motion. If the country is to lose an independent judiciary, it will, we believe, be because it would have first lost an independent Senate. A long step, a very long step, would have been taken away from our system of checks and balances.

Influential papers in London and other British cities have expressed approval of the President's plans. That is understandable — it is a step toward a system of government with which they are familiar. We very earnestly hope that there may be good, and better, relations between the two democracies. But let it frankly be recognized that the two systems of government are different, and substantially different. Whether one system or the other is preferable is a matter upon which opinions differ. If the British people desire to have a democracy without checks and balances, that is for them to say. If the American people desire to have a democracy with checks and balances, that is for them to say.

Which system of government do the American people desire? It is a tremendous issue. It is not a partisan issue. It is not an economic issue. It is a system-of-government issue. Shall or shall there not be this long step taken away from our system of checks and balances? We believe it to be the most tremendous issue, unconnected with a war, which has ever arisen in this country.

To return to the President's parable. The three horses could not of themselves plow the field. There must be a driver, and a driver prepared to use a whip if necessary. Where is the driver to be found? In his Victory Banquet address, the President revealed himself. Let not your heart be troubled. I will be the driver; I will supply the whip.

The reaction of the country was not what the President had expected. He realized too late the implications of his parable. He sought to explain it away. But he did protest too much. By his own parable shall ye judge him.

In the name of American democracy the President is proposing something which will undermine the foundations of American democracy. We have now the Supreme Court of the United States. The adoption of the President's proposals would swiftly lead to the substitution of the Supreme Will of a Single Individual.

Problems we have, but the way to solve them is not by declaring American democracy bankrupt and passing to what would be, in substance, a new system of government.

Very truly yours,

EDWARD H. WARREN
JOSEPH WARREN
MORTON C. CAMPBELL

'WE SHALL WIN'

THE preceding item has shown me arrayed against President Roosevelt. But I am not of those who view all things through 'I-hate-Roosevelt' glasses. To the amazement of many, I worked and voted for him in 1940. Some of those who had sworn *by* me in 1937 swore *at* me in 1940.

I was bred in a community where many regarded it as a badge of respectability to go to church every Lord's Day, and to vote the straight Republican ticket every election day. And as a boy I greatly admired Abraham Lincoln (and later grew to appraise him as one of the greatest men that ever lived in any country). My first vote for a presidential nominee was cast for McKinley in 1896, and all my life I have usually (although by no means always) voted for Republican nominees. There has been in my mind a prima-facie case for any nominee who had the Republican label. But a prima-facie case (as there is often occasion to emphasize to students) is *only* a prima-facie case, and every such case is open to the possibility of rebuttal. In 1940, the prima-facie case in my mind for the Republican presidential nominees was rebutted.

If there had been no issues other than domestic issues, there were various pros and cons. For President Roosevelt were: (1) the courage, boldness, and effectiveness with which he tackled the job in 1933, for which the country owes him gratitude; (2) his *ideals* of a more equitable distribution of wealth; (3) the so-called Wall Street legislation, something like which had long been needed.

Against him were: (1) his tendency to demand that Congressmen should be docile 'President-men' which was rapidly undermining the Constitutional plan that there should be a check upon the Executive through a Congress composed of think-it-out-myself members; (2) his attack on the independence of the judiciary evidenced by his Supreme Court plan; (3) a swollen and inefficient bureaucracy; once Congress legislated; now it was being asked again and again to make partial abdications by delegation to administrative bodies the members of which were nominated by the President; some of these bodies — notably the S.E.C. — had, I think, given a good account of themselves, but there were others of these bodies of which that could not justifiably be said; they had great powers which, it is true, were supposed to be subject to judicial supervision, but this did not amount to much, for the Court was powerless to interfere unless the administrative body was *plainly* wrong, and some of the members of such bodies were persons of, at best, mediocre ability, who, flushed with power, did not, so to speak, carry their liquor well and were much inclined to regard themselves as a law to themselves and to act without due consideration and to proceed in a more or less arbitrary manner; (4) the undermining of the respect of the community for the Puritan virtues of working hard and saving (and I am a Puritan or nothing); (5) national financing which seemed to me not to rest upon enduring foundations; (6) the utilization of what I think may fairly be characterized as a vicious-circle political policy, — tax, spend, elect; and (7) the disregard of the tradition against three terms.

If the election had been concerned solely with domestic issues, it would have seemed clear to me, after balancing the pros and cons, that a change of administration would be of benefit to the nation.

But the domestic issues were *not* the sole issues. I happened to be in England in the summer of 1939, and to have listened in on the radio when Prime Minister Chamberlain told his listeners that they were at war with Germany. I did not like that address a little bit. Over there they were up against something tremendous, and I had the gravest doubt whether the Prime Minister had what it would take to give adequate leadership. There was no bugle call.

If Germany won, how about my own country? The German people really believed that they were a superstock, and that they could, and would, dominate the world. That was as clear to me as the sun on a cloudless noon. Hitler's greatest hold on the German people was the fact that he was promising to accomplish their hearts' desire. 'Deutschland über Alles' was to them more than the name of a song.

If the British Empire collapsed, the Nazis would attack my own country just as soon as they could get around to it (meanwhile making as many Americans as possible believe that there was no danger of such an attack).

When, not long after war was declared in 1939, I crossed the Atlantic homeward bound, I was feeling pretty blue about the future of the United States. On the liner there were numerous Smoke Room Parliaments where the war and its effect on the United States were discussed. I did not participate — there were plenty who were eager to talk — but I listened.

One of the other passengers was a man in a very important

position in national affairs. He was loud in his admiration for the Nazis; we could 'do business,' very profitable business, with them; our hope lay in not rubbing them the wrong way, but in laying foundations for cordial cooperation. He was as guileless as the serpent and as wise as the dove.

The extent to which such thoughts seemed to be persuasive with other passengers amazed and jolted me.

Back at work in Cambridge, I grew more and more uneasy. I found so many persons (who had always led blameless lives of conscious rectitude) doing the ostrich act, — refusing to look ugly facts in the face, even opposing swift and adequate measures to avert the peril. They did not listen. They scoffed at me as an alarmist. There are none so blind as those who have the will not to see. They were so positive, and so wrong.

But President Roosevelt had vision. He saw early, and he saw clearly, the extent of the peril. He sought to give a vigorous, effective leadership. I made up my mind that it was a time to put first things first; that the safety of the country was the first thing; that he had the right sow by the ear; and that, however much I differed from him on domestic issues, the thing for me to do was to work and vote for his re-election.

I take solid satisfaction in feeling that my vote for him cancelled the vote of some Nazi sympathizer or appeaser who usually voted Democratic, but in 1940 voted Republican.

That 1940 election was really a good deal closer than most people seem to realize. Analyze the returns. Eliminate Texas, where the result was a foregone conclusion. If the votes in all other states having sixteen or more electoral votes are considered, pou will find that a shift of about five hundred thousand votes distributed through those states would have given the election to Mr. Willkie. I believe that President Roosevelt would not have been re-elected had there not been at least five hundred thousand voters who, like myself, usually voted Republican, but this time voted Democratic.

Let me say that Mr. Willkie's undiluted, vigorous patriotism seems to me to be above all question. I have no doubt that, if he had been elected, he would have done the best he could to save the country. But his supporters were heterogeneous. I believe that the Nazi sympathizers and appeasers voted, practically *en masse*, for him. Many of his supporters were, I fully realize, of the salt of the earth, *but* many of his supporters were of the pepper of Hell.

If he had been elected, there would, almost certainly, have been divided councils and hesitant, uncertain action. I am very glad that President Roosevelt was re-elected and that I contributed my bit to that result.

If Mr. Willkie had been elected, Herr Hitler would have smiled a sneering, sadist smile and would have made a Puckish observation: 'What fools these Americans are.'

After Pearl Harbor, I ran into many persons with long faces, who were taking it out in moaning. Pearl Harbor fathers, who were terrified at the cries of their offspring. This moved me to write a letter to the *New York Herald Tribune* under the *nom de plume* 'Civis Americanus Sum.' I was speaking, not as a member of any law faculty, but as an American citizen.

When I wrote that, I had no intent to have it published except in my favorite New York paper. But some persons who agreed with me both in 1937 and 1940 spotted my authorship and urged me to have the letter published in other papers also. Thereupon I amplified it into the form given below, and it has been published in numerous American papers, and also in the *Montreal Gazette*. I have sent a copy (in the slightly abbreviated form in which it appeared on March 21 in the *Harvard Alumni Bulletin*) to every student in the Harvard Law School whose studies have been interrupted by his becoming a member of the armed forces of the United States.

To look ahead. I am proud of being an American. We are a bit slow on starting, but, once we put our hand to the plow, we see the furrow through. We are a long way from furrow's end. As I write, I think that there is a good deal of danger that the people will feel that the tide has definitely turned and will become overoptimistic. Do not underrate the strength and tenacity of our enemies. Keep your eye on Europe. The Nazis must be *smashed*. There must be no return this time of German soldiers to welcoming, cheering, flowers-scattering crowds. Otherwise we shall have to do it all over again. Everybody makes mistakes, but to make the *same* mistake twice is the badge of the damfool. Prussia, producer and purveyor of poisonous, Prussic psychology, must be segregated. Once victory is won in Europe, the Japanese will, with the aid of the Chinese, be overcome. Asia for the Asiatics, but let the Asiatics be decent, live-withable people.

To the Editor of ——:

I make no prophecy, I make no guess, as to how long the fighting will last. It will be some fight. But I have a thought-out confidence that we shall win the triple war. The bases of that confidence are much more solid, much more reliable, much more fit to endure than wistful thinking. They are as follows:

1. We are a united people. Among the vaunted Nazi assets was the Berlin Psychological Academy. The leader, 'twas said, had gathered about him the most remarkable group of remarkable psychological experts that had ever been assembled. Every plan was submitted to them, and they gave advice — expertissimo advice — on the precise effect which the execution of any plan would have upon the minds of the German people, and also upon the minds of the people in other countries.

The epic episode at Pearl Harbor was the most colossal psychological blunder in the recorded history of mankind.

2. We are a resourceful people. We have immense quantities of raw materials; we have immense plants, well equipped and well organized; we have millions of free men of brawn and skill who work with their hands *and* brains. True it is that Hitler has millions of men working for him, but they are slaves. The members of American labor unions who work with their hands and brains are today almost to a man keen — very keen — to show, and to show clearly, that the productive capacity of free labor is far greater than the productive capacity of slave labor. And, moreover (and this may prove to be very important), we have a large number of hard-thinking, long-headed, shrewd men with the Yankee flair for invention who will produce (perhaps have already produced) some devices which when put in action will make the Axis wonder where out of Heaven or Hell *that* came from.

We have the raw materials; we have the plants; we have the money; we have the men; we have or shall have the inventions; *and* (put the emphasis on the 'and') we have the guts.

The combination of all those resources will forge a colossal battering ram which will smash the Axis. 'Smash' is the word. Nothing else but. When the Axis started a mechanized war, they walked right up the American alley.

3. We are a people with a sense of humor. Few Germans in Germany have a sense of humor. But most Americans have it, — have plenty. We have an eye for the funny side of things. We relish a good joke even when it is on us. A sense of humor is a wonderful shock absorber. Bring on your reverses, you Axis. We'll take them. We'll grin and bear it. We shall bear it *because* we shall grin.

If a man has a sense of humor, you may get him down, but you cannot put him out.

A man naturally credits other men with having the same instincts and motives which he himself has. We are a decent, peace-loving nation, and it has been very hard — almost impossible — for us to realize that there are other nations in the world (which science is steadily compressing into a smaller, more compact world) which are not decent and peace-loving, but, on the contrary, follow the lead, and even enthusiastically follow the lead, of men who worship the Devil of War, and despise and ridicule the God in Whom the great bulk of the American people believe and trust (although worshipping Him in varying ways).

This is a death struggle — make no mistake about that — between, on the one hand, nations which for many years have been planning and preparing for total war as a means of chaining other nations to their triumphal juggernaut car, and, on the other hand, nations which during those same years have devoted themselves to the pursuits, profits, and pleasures of peace.

On such facts, it is inevitable that the warlike nations shall obtain initial advantages, — and substantial initial advantages at that. Let us look squarely in the face the unpleasant fact that, in all probability, we are in for more initial reverses, — very likely serious initial reverses.

The Axis Powers always start with showing how good they are at giving it, but later, as the tide turns, they are not so good at taking it. At the start we shall have to take it, chins up, teeth clenched, fists closed. But later we shall get around to giving it, and when that time comes, we shall give it in a way that will make eruptive volcanoes pale into insignificance.

Hitler's sun has passed its meridian. The legend of his 'all-wise' leadership, of invincibility, no longer has its magnetic drawing power. He missed the boat in June, 1940. Russia has taught him that, however crushing may be the tactics of a bully toward small nations, the success of such tactics against a large nation is something different. But even if his sun sinks below the horizon, that will not be the end of our troubles.

The root of the evil goes much deeper. It goes down to Bismarck's 'Blood and Iron.' If Hitler is purged in his turn, power in Germany will be seized by the army caste, and that caste just cannot comprehend the fundamental American ideal of 'Live and let live' to be applied between nations as well as between citizens.

As for the Japanese. They now are loudly crowing, announcing the Rising Sun. But night always follows day. Night awaits them, and the night will be black.

CIVIS AMERICANUS SUM

January 5, 1941

Chapter Five

BEHIND THE HARVARD GATES

BURNING POLITICAL QUESTIONS
STATEMENT AT A MEETING OF THE LAW FACULTY

THE question is: 'To what extent is it proper for a member of the Harvard Law School Faculty to speak or write in public on a burning public question, and to call attention when so doing to his connection with the School, thereby inevitably using the prestige of the School to add weight and to give persuasiveness to his opinion with the public?'

I have had occasion in the past to do some very hard, and very prolonged, thinking on this matter. The results of that thinking have lain in the bottle for many years. The time has come to uncork the bottle.

There seems to me to be a clear distinction between (1) the liberty of thought and speech which is to be accorded to a professor with reference to any matter which lies within the scope of the course or courses which he is entrusted to give, and (2) the liberty of speech which he may properly use with reference to a burning public question lying outside that scope.

As to the first, there is no difficulty. It is fundamental that a professor should be given absolute liberty to express the conclusions he has reached after honest and thorough thinking, and his reasons for reaching those conclusions (of course, in language without Billingsgate offensiveness). He must not be exposed to even the slightest fear that the full and frank expression of his conclusions and reasons, whatever they are, may endanger the security of his tenure.

As to the second, there is much difficulty. Should he refrain altogether from using the prestige of this Law School to aid him in the propagation of his own views on a burning public question?

Although the prestige of the School is a collective asset, my answer is 'No.'

A professor does not, or should not, become an intellectual monk. There is no great gulf between this School and the outside world.

On the other hand, I submit that there should be some limitation; the difficulty is to express that limitation. I am unable to find any formula that can express that limitation with anything even approaching the certainty of a mathematical formula (with its connotation of completeness and finality). The best that I can do is to say that recognition should be given to two conceptions, the due recognition of *both* of which will tend to a poise, a balance:

One is the conception of '*Liberté*'; the other is the conception of '*Liberté oblige.*' The professor in using his liberty should be sensitive to the thought of '*Liberté oblige.*' The professor should always be sure that his heart is in the work of the School, — that he is not serving two masters, the School *and* his outside causes. He should be careful to guard the interests of the School, always remembering that the public is likely to confuse individuals with institutions, and he should have a just realization of the probable reaction of his utterances upon the School.

But, in the last analysis, it must be treated as a question of conscience, to be determined by each professor according to his own conscience. The restraint should be a voluntary internal restraint rather than a compulsory external restraint. The School must take some risk. I think, if any generalization can be made, it is that the professor should *incline* against doing something which will in all probability have the effect of using the prestige of the School to add weight and to give persuasiveness to his own views on burning public questions. He should be slow to do so, — should rarely do so.

It is not to be expected that there will be no occasions when some one of us will regret, and be inclined to censure, the utterance of some colleague upon a question of burning public interest. Let us all remember that the men on this Faculty hold a great variety of opinions. If we look at the outside world, array men according to their opinions, or lack of opinions, and read from left to right, one finds Bolsheviks, Radicals, Progressives, Pussyfooters, Moderates, Conservatives, and die-hard Tories. If the character of the Faculty were ever challenged, and I was asked to be of counsel for the defense, I should deny that we had any

Bolsheviks, Pussyfooters, or die-hard Tories. But we certainly stock the other varieties, and can at a moment's notice supply any brand required. And I regard that as desirable, not deplorable.

Let us be particularly chary of denouncing a colleague as having given evidence of bias in what he says. All men are biased. We are all born biased, and we continue to be biased throughout our lives. There are no men without bias, except dead men. We all try to act without bias, but none of us makes a complete success of that. If any man on this Faculty is to be condemned for bias, let him who is without bias cast the first stone.

But I will, in closing, permit myself to say that those who are so enthusiastically in favor of some specific proposal that they incline to construe opposition as evidence of bias should realize that there may be a bias 'for,' as well as a bias 'against.'

THE HARVARD LAW SCHOOL IN
THE FIRST GREAT WAR

Harvard Law School Year Book, 1941–42

In 1916–17, there were 857 students (66 more than in the previous year). In 1917–18, the number fell from 857 to 297; in 1918–19, from 297 to 128. The light guttered, flickered, but did not go out.

In December, 1918, announcement was made of a special session of seven months (February to August, 1919). The intent was to save, so to speak, a year of their lives to students who had been honorably discharged from the services. Three hundred and seven students came to this special session.

In 1919–20, the number of students bounded back again to 883.

The Faculty in 1916–17 was only about a third as large as it now is, — the President, the Dean, and ten other members. Three have died; President Lowell and Professors Williston and Beale have become Emeritus; Dean Pound has, as Dean, become Emeritus, but as a University professor still gives an important part of his time to the School; Professor Frankfurter has become the fifth man who has both taught in the Harvard Law School and has also been a Justice of the Supreme Court.

Joseph Warren, Scott, Chafee, and I were the other members of the 1916–17 Faculty.

In the special session of 1919, the courses offered were: First year, Procedure, Contracts, Criminal Law and Principles of Liability, Property, Torts; second year, Agency, Bills and Notes, Equity, Evidence, Property, Sales; third year, Conflict of Laws, Constitutional Law, Corporations, Equity, Public Utilities, Trusts. From February to June, 1919, when the School was a double-barrelled school, most of the courses were given in the special session by the same men who gave them in the regular session.

Throughout the war years there was no resolution by the Faculty on any matter relating to the war which was not, after discussion and moulding, voted unanimously.

The resolutions adopted included the following (April 24, 1917):

1. *Third-Year Students*. Third-year students actually in the service of the United States or actually called into the service of the United States prior to the end of the school year, including such students as shall be accepted in federal training camps, will be excused from residence from the date at which they are so actually called into service or accepted in training camps, and, if their record at the present date is such that, if continued, they would be recommended for a degree in June, 1917, they will be recommended therefor.

2. *Second-Year Students*. Any second-year student in full and regular standing actually called into the service of the United States, as above defined, now or before the end of the school year, will be excused from residence from the date at which he is so actually called into service. Such students may return and complete their third year, and if they take successfully all their third-year examinations, such examinations will also be accepted in lieu of second-year examinations.

3. *First-Year Students*. Any first-year student who has been in regular attendance up to the date of his actual calling into the service of the United States, as above defined, who is so called into the service prior to the end of the school year, will be excused from residence from the date at which he is so actually called into service. Such students may return and complete their second year, and if they take successfully all their second-year examinations, such examinations will also be accepted in lieu of first-year examinations.

A word as to the financial wherewithal. In 1916–17, more than two thirds of the income was from tuition. In the next two years there was, of course, a sharp break in such income. Nevertheless, the surplus of the School (the amount standing to its credit on the books of the Treasurer of the Corporation under the heading 'General Suspense') increased from $73,837.96 on June 30, 1917, to $79,590.30 on June 30, 1919. Several factors contributed to this result, — Austin Hall was leased to the United States Naval Radio School for $43,750; the members of the Faculty who served in the special session desired to receive therefor only an amount in the nature of an honorarium; and in the front office there was an Aberdeen watch over every item of expenditure, no matter how trivial. Expenditure for the Library was cut, but only by about twelve per cent.

The state of mind of some (not most) citizens in the present emergency is disquieting. There are some who are conscious of what they owe the country; and there are some who, like an ostrich, refuse to face ugly facts. Persons who assert that, under present world conditions, our democracy will not prove fit to survive (in the Darwinian sense of the phrase) are obviously a menace. But persons who assert, with complacent optimism and bland, indulgent smile, that there is no danger are also a menace, — and probably a greater menace.

I am confident that at least ninety per cent of the men who are, or have been, students in the Harvard Law School will size up the facts with common sense and shrewdness; that they realize that disabling, crippling, hamstringing the nation would of course undermine the security and prosperity of its members; and that they will grimly and effectively do their parts to prevent such hamstringing. And General Grim will do it.

To look ahead. A nation with no ideals will decline and fall. But man cannot live on ideals alone. There is need also of the realistic approach to the difficult task of implementing the ideals. *Ideals inadequately blended with realism do much more harm than good.* Let us look squarely in the face the fact that in the last thirty years we have shown more capacity for generating enthusiasm for ideals than for finding effective ways to realize them. We have scaled peaks of enthusiasm only to slip and plunge down into a slough of despond, — disillusioned and cynical. If we are to live and be happy about it, we cannot afford to do that sort of thing indefinitely. When this emergency is over there ought to be a lot of common-sense, hard-headed, clear, simple, modest thinking. *A child can grasp an ideal. But only wise men can implement it.* Wisdom is the principal thing; therefore get wisdom; and with all thy getting, get understanding. We must think out practical, workable ways and means for implementing the fundamental American ideal of 'Live and let live' to be applied to nations.

But the immediate job is (as I see it) the elementary job of self-preservation.

THE HARVARD LAW SCHOOL OUTLOOK IN NOVEMBER, 1941

STATEMENT MADE AT A MEETING, NOVEMBER 23, 1941, OF THE
VISITING COMMITTEE OF THE HARVARD LAW SCHOOL

Mr. Chairman and Gentlemen:

I have had printed what I wish to say, and will read it. I have not shown this to, or talked about it with, anyone else, — not even Dean Landis. The sole responsibility for it is upon me.

The primary function of this School is, I submit, to equip young men so that they may be useful and successful members of the bar, — about one third of the time to be devoted to giving them useful information and about two thirds to training their minds so that they can give a good account of themselves in tackling *any* legal problem. This is a large job, and it is very difficult to do that job excellently. This School for many years devoted itself exclusively to that, and it came to be recognized as *facile princeps* among American law schools *because* throughout some decades it did do that job, and did do it excellently. The pick of the young legal brains of the country came to this School, came to it eagerly, and went away enthusiastic over the training they had received.

In the last quarter of a century we have taken on other things. Dean Pound thought the School should also take the lead in what is often called 'higher legal education,' and I will use that expression, stating, however, that I put those three words in quotation marks. Dean Pound talked with me fully about his ideals and they seemed to me to merit most careful consideration.

But one of the fundamentals in my thinking is that while, on the one hand, ideals are essential to progressive development, yet, on the other hand, there must be the realistic approach to the difficult task of implementing those ideals, *and* that ideals not adequately blended with realism do more harm, much more harm, than good. Therefore I pondered, and pondered long, over Dean Pound's ideals.

I had some fear that the School might be more or less like the dog in the fable who was carrying a large leg of mutton in his mouth and who on crossing a bridge saw his own reflection in the water and thought he saw another dog carrying a much larger leg of mutton, and thereupon dropped his own leg of mutton into the river in order to get the larger leg of mutton. And eventually I made two suggestions to Dean Pound. The first was that it should be recognized as the fundamental of fundamentals that the School was to remain *primarily* a professional school (devoted to fitting young men for the practice of the law) as contrasted with what I called, for the lack of a better term, an Academy of Jurisprudence; that the undergraduate courses were to remain the chief object of interest and were to be treasured as the chief source of its strength, and that there should be no blurring of that fundamental. The second was that since the bulk of our income came from tuition paid by undergraduates — at that time more than two thirds was so derived — it should be recognized that it was equitable that such income should be devoted to undergraduate purposes. Dean Pound expressed himself as being in entire accord with me on both points.

I am satisfied — let there be no misunderstanding or shadow of misunderstanding about this — that Dean Pound sought with complete sincerity to realize his ideals as to 'higher legal education' within the limits of the two safeguards mentioned above. I further believe that it always lay in his mind that there had been no disregard of either of these two safeguards, and certainly his own conduct of undergraduate courses continued at the same high level at which it had always been.

But little by little, the centre of gravity shifted. Just what caused that is matter of opinion. I attribute it largely to the connotations inherent in that adjective 'higher' in that phrase 'higher legal education.' If there is a 'higher' legal education, that means there is a 'lower' legal education, and it is natural that men should be keen to be associated with the 'higher' branch. It seems to me clear that a considerable number of the members of the Faculty did come to take a greater interest, enthusiasm, and pride in graduate courses than in undergraduate courses. There were some who regarded those courses as the chief glory of the School, and were perhaps just a bit inclined to look upon the 'rudimentary' courses with good-natured tolerance.

Contrast this attitude with the attitude of Dean Ames. After I had served on the Faculty as an assistant professor for three years, he said that my work had been such that he felt that I was qualified to be entrusted with a first-year course, and offered me Property I. And I well remember that President Eliot congratulated me on my promotion.

Now, let us consider the effect of the diversion of interest to graduate courses away from undergraduate courses, — to 'higher legal education' from 'lower legal education.'

How much good has been accomplished? The number of students who have been attracted has been small. Last year we had twenty-five resident graduate students out of a total enrolment of 1248. So much as to quantity. How about quality of students? The graduate courses have attracted a certain number of really tip-top men. I do not belittle that. But they have also attracted a certain number of men of a different calibre. Some of these have been men who have been inclined to shrink from the ordeal of practice, who have obtained from us some second degree and on the faith of that have obtained a teaching appointment in some other law school. I have not in recent years followed carefully the personnel of graduate students, but I did follow it carefully and in detail up to my resignation in 1929, and I became convinced that we were giving a 'higher' degree to some men who could not by any possibility have won our LL.B. *cum laude* and who would have had a great deal of difficulty in satisfying our requirements even for a pass degree. I do not believe that such men are a source of much strength to the nation, and I believe that sending such men out into the world with our label for a 'higher' degree has tended not to increase, but to decrease, our prestige.

In a word, we have had a mixed bag. Some good, but some definitely poor. Whether on balance we have strengthened, or weakened, our prestige is a question.

But now consider the effect of this diversion of interest upon our reputation as the School where young men could get a training for the practice of the law unequalled by the training given in any other law school.

The time when we were *facile princeps* among American law schools has gone with the wind. Geography has never been our ally, — it is not for us, but against us. It is vital that we should not become just another good law school, — if we do, geography will beat us.

The Harvard Law School magnet has ceased to draw with its old compelling force. We no longer have the pick of the young legal brains of the country. I have been disturbed, deeply disturbed, at seeing how many students of the calibre we are keen to obtain have of recent years turned elsewhere. This is true even of some sons of fathers who were our graduates and who were, on leaving the School, enthusiastic about the School. No doubt this is to a considerable extent the result of the fact that numerous other schools have become definitely better schools than they formerly were; but it is also to a considerable extent the result of the fact that there is a belief that the School has taken on too many things; that it has ceased to put the effort that it used to put into the training of young men to become useful and successful members of the bar; that a good many members of the Faculty are rather more interested in other things; and that the School has become topheavy, with too much sail and too little ballast. Such thoughts about the School are, I believe, more widespread, much more widespread, than most of you realize.

Now, what are we going to do about it?

I digress to speak of the years 1917–19.

At the request of the editors of the *Harvard Law School Year Book* for 1941–42, I have written an article on the School in the First Great War. One paragraph is substantially as follows:

A word as to the financial wherewithal. In 1916–17 over two thirds of the income was derived from tuition. In the following two years there was, of course, a sharp drop in such income. Nevertheless, the surplus of the School increased from about $76,000 on June 30, 1917, to about $79,000 on June 30, 1919. Several factors contributed to this result, — Austin Hall was leased to the United States Naval Radio School for $43,750; the members of the Faculty who served in the special session in 1919 desired to receive therefor only a payment in the nature of an honorarium; and there was a front-office Aberdeen watch on every item of expenditure, no matter how trivial. Expenditure for the Library was cut, but only by about twelve per cent.

That the surplus did not sharply decrease in 1917–19, but actually even increased a bit, is remarkable. No such happy result in the years immediately ahead is to be expected. We already have a substantial deficit, and, so far as I can see, that deficit will inevitably increase.

I suppose that the Corporation will, within limits, finance the School, but that sort of thing cannot go on indefinitely. In the last resort, if we are ever to get once more on a sound financial basis, the greatest asset of this School will prove to be the good will of those students who have obtained here the foundation of their success, often a very substantial success, in after life. The response of such men to the appeal for funds for the 'higher legal education' and for an enlarged plant fell much below expectation. But I have the faith to believe, and do believe, that their response to an appeal for funds to make good a deficit caused by keeping the undergraduate courses at a high pitch of efficiency in the present emergency would yield substantial results.

I am not urging that our curriculum should remain as it was in, say, 1910, the last year of the administration of Dean Ames. Do not misunderstand me on that. That was an excellent curriculum for the conditions then existing. But conditions changed, and greatly changed. Courts came to be occupied more and more with decisions in public law. In 1936, it was proposed that our curriculum should be overhauled to meet the new conditions, so as to give public law a greater portion of the time as contrasted with private law. There was a full and free discussion in the Faculty, — the discussion was a good example of what a Faculty discussion ought to be. Of course there had to be a good deal of give and take, and I suppose that the final result did not precisely suit anyone. But I thought that, on the main question, the Faculty hit it just about right in the new division of time between public law and private law. We may have to do that sort of thing again.

I am aware of the fact that a man sixty-eight years old is apt to incline to think that things were done better when he was young. But I ask you all not to shrug off what I am saying on that ground. In preparing this statement, I have been keenly conscious of that danger and believe that nothing I am saying can be, with justification, attributed to any such inclination.

I will close by speaking of 'scholarship.' It is axiomatic that no man is a fit member of this Faculty unless he is a scholar and treasures scholarship. But a large stock of information, unleavened by other qualities, does not make a scholar, a wide-spread opinion to the contrary notwithstanding. The three members of this Faculty who contributed most to moulding my mind were Ames, pre-eminently a stimulating man; Gray, pre-eminently a reliable man; and the elder Thayer, pre-eminently a wise man. I have consciously sought to fashion all my Faculty activities on a model which was a composite of Ames and Gray and Thayer, and am convinced that I could not have found a better model. All three read much, discussed much, pondered most, and wrote a little, — but only a little. I have collected everything (except case books) in our library written by them, — every treatise, every article, every book review, every address. Ames served thirty-seven years, and wrote about six hundred pages; Gray served forty-two years, and wrote about fifteen hundred pages; Thayer served twenty-nine years, and wrote about fourteen hundred pages. Their combined writings would not fill more than two thirds of a one-foot bookshelf.

I emphasize the fact that, in decades when the School was *facile princeps* among American law schools, the writings of these three famous members of its Faculty work out at an average per year per man of less than twelve pages.

Precious as their writings were, the greatest value of those three men to the School was in something other than their writings. Their writings could be read by anyone without coming to the School. The spoken word is, at least with students, much more effective, much more stimulating, much more inspiring, than the written word. The spoken word is alive, there is a possibility for nuances and suggestive hints and inflections which cannot be translated into cold print. The most precious result of the scholarly activities of Ames and Gray and Thayer was in the ideals which seeped out of them into those who studied under them and which their students imbibed more unconsciously than consciously. Virtue went out of those three into their students. They breathed the breath of intellectual life, and a wholesome intellectual life, into many a man who until he came under them had been only a lump of mental clay.

Our problem differs in kind (and not merely in degree) from the problems in some other parts of the University. Take physics, or chemistry, or medicine. There the members of a Faculty are concerned with the laws of nature. Man can neither make these laws nor unmake them; they are immutable, and man can only discover and apply them. But law is man-made. The ancient but forever recurring question is what rules are *wise* in the light of the experience of the past and in view of the conditions of the present. The opinion of any one man at any one time is only a slight factor in determining that. I believe in historical legal research, and in paying due respect to the past, and have spent many of the happiest hours of my life in communion with the Plantagenet judges and Coke; but knowledge of the past is only a part, and, in my opinion, by no means the most important part, of the proper equipment of a member of any law faculty. It is noteworthy that Holmes in his later life came to feel that the value of historical legal research might easily be overestimated. Such research does not discover an immutable, eternal law of nature. It only discovers a man-made law which at best was a wise rule in conditions as they existed when the rule was laid down, and which may prove misleading, rather than helpful, if applied under present conditions. Therefore, since the opinion of any one man at any one time is only a slight factor, what the nation needs, if it is to have wise laws, is that there should be many, many citizens competent to make, or to contribute in making, rules which are both sensible and workable. And the chief value to the nation of Ames and Gray and Thayer was not in their writings, but was in the character of the minds of thousands of students who under them acquired intellectual acumen and intellectual conscience, and who passed from their studies here to participate in the practice of the law and not infrequently to serve in legislatures or on the bench. Such men were the chief glory of the School.

I have no disposition to belittle our large and splendid plant, or our large and splendid library, or our large and splendid Faculty. I have tried to express my thoughts in such a manner that the manner of expression would wound the susceptibilities of no one, but, even if I have not succeeded in that, I beseech you all to approach this problem with a humble spirit and an open mind, and to ponder these two questions:

First: Is it not to the best interests of the School that there should be relatively more attention given to undergraduate courses and less to graduate courses than is now given; and also that there should be a substantial increase in research and enthusiasm in and for the fine art of stimulating, reliable, wise, oral teaching as contrasted with a productivity measured by writing?

Second: Is it not to the best interests of the School that in the present emergency the undergraduate courses should be maintained at an even higher level of efficiency than the present level, so that there may be a basis for our recapturing the prestige we once enjoyed of being clearly *the* best law school in the United States for training young men to be useful and successful members of the bar?

AN OPENING LECTURE IN PROPERTY I

WE ARE scheduled to have ninety-one lectures. About two thirds of these will be devoted to discussion of specific cases; about one third to mere exposition by me. In the lectures devoted to exposition, I shall move at such a pace that most of you will be unable to appreciate the full significance of the exposition simply by listening. For most of ·you it will be wise (1) to take full notes, and (2) to read and ponder (mark that word), ponder over these notes shortly thereafter.

These are preliminary lectures. But they will not be devoted to glittering generalities or innocuous platitudes. I shall try at once to get to grips with important, fundamental matters, and also to let you see an arc of my mental circle. We're off.

Law is a term often used with a very broad scope, as equivalent to a rule, — any rule. We speak of the laws of etiquette, of the laws of contract bridge. But law is also a term often used in a much more restricted sense, — connoting rules which may conveniently be called legal (or, if you prefer the word, juristic) rules. When we speak of this School as a Law School, we are using the term in the restricted sense. We shall be concerned only with legal rules.

Now, what is the scope of legal rules? Thousands of pages have been written upon that by jurists. Just what is the answer is still controversial, — highly controversial. My own answer is as follows: A legal rule is a rule designed to define what ought to be done, or ought not be done (1) as between the sovereign and those legal units who owe obedience to it; (2) as between such legal units themselves; and (3) as between one sovereign and/or those who owe obedience to it, and another sovereign and/or those who owe obedience to such other sovereign.

Laws defining crimes and taxes are examples of legal rules of the first class, — public law. Laws of property, contracts, and torts are examples of legal rules of the second class, — private law. Treaties are examples of legal rules of the third class, — international law.

No rule is a legal rule unless it is backed by a political sovereign. Every legal rule has the might of a political sovereign behind it. The test is not as to whether those affected do, or do not, usually abide by the rules. Some social rules often are obeyed more fully than some legal rules. Thus, if you say to a man that he is a lawbreaker, it may well be that he will be, not offended, but rather pleased, — that he will be delighted with his own delinquencies. But if you say to him that he is not always a gentleman, he will probably never again regard you as a friend. The test is not even whether there is any legal sanction for the rule. Some rules laid down by constitutions and many rules laid down by international law have no legal sanction. The test is, I submit, solely whether the rule is laid down by a political sovereign or by some delegate or agent of a political sovereign.

This, let me make it clear, is only my own answer. Other answers have been made. Ponder my answer. It is laid before you, not for docile acceptance, but for consideration. My intent is only to *start* your thinking, — to give you something definite to shoot at.

Now a minor point. I used the expression 'legal units.' I think you will, throughout your studies in this School and even throughout your practice, find that a convenient phrase. A legal unit is, I submit, anything which in the eyes of the law may acquire a right or become subject to a duty.

There are four different kinds of legal units. First, human beings are *usually* legal units — although slaves are not, and monks may not be. Second, all *incorporated* bodies of human beings are legal units. In this country today legislative sanction is indispensable to incorporation. That legislative sanction may be given by special act, under some circumstances, whereby named human beings are incorporated, but is usually given by general acts permitting incorporation by compliance with defined conditions. Third, bodies of men, not incorporated, are *sometimes* treated as legal units by the courts without legislative sanction therefor. This raises problems of great practical importance and also of great intellectual difficulty. I have written a long treatise on that, entitled *Corporate Advantages Without Incorporation*. I have had it said to me that there is a headache in every page. It does not seem to me to be quite so bad as that, but it is no doubt a stiff book. As a question of timing, I recommend to most of you that you do *not* tackle it in this first year of your studies, but that you do tackle it before you leave the School. It is sufficient now to say that there are certainly many decided cases, the natural explanation of which is that the courts have felt at liberty to treat, at least for some purposes, an unincorporated body of human beings as a legal unit, although there is no legislative sanction therefor. Fourth, there are, I think, a few cases where there are legal units which are neither human beings nor bodies of human beings. Popularly speaking, the estate of a deceased person is a unit, with *its* rights and *its* obligations. I regret to say that the common law does *not* confirm the popular view on that, although there are some statutes which do. I shall have occasion to refer later quite fully to what in the eye of the law does happen to the rights and obligations of a human being on his death.

Now, to come back from this diversion to the main stream of thought. I have given you my definition of a legal rule. Use that, tentatively. You will have occasion during your studies in this School to consider at least six kinds of legal rules:

1. The provisions of the Constitution of the United States. Here the sovereign, the people of the whole nation, is itself laying down rules.

2. The provisions of treaties made by the United States with other nations. By treaties rules are laid down which are part of the supreme law of the land. The treaties are backed by the word of the United States.

3. The provisions of the constitution of a state. Here the sovereign, the people of a particular state, is itself laying down rules. We have dual sovereignty, — the United States is a sovereign, and each state is also a sovereign.

4. Statutes. Power of laying down rules is delegated by the sovereign, national or state, to defined legislatures which pass statutes.

5. Rules and regulations laid down by bodies, inferior in dignity to legislatures, pursuant to authority vested in them by constitutions and/or statutes. Thus, a legislature may authorize a municipal corporation to pass ordinances for the regulation of traffic. Thus, Congress has set up important administrative bodies, such as the Tariff Commission, the Interstate Commerce Commission, the Securities and Exchange Commission, and the National Labor Board, and has authorized them to lay down

rules and regulations. I view a legislature as a delegate of the sovereign, and an administrative body as a sub-delegate of the sovereign.

6. Rules laid down by courts. The early English judges were the king's delegates or agents. Our judges today are the delegates or agents of the sovereign people.

The rules laid down by legislatures in statutes, by administrative bodies in ordinances or rules and regulations, and by judges in decisions, all stem from sovereignty, — all have the might of a political sovereign behind them.

Now, in this course we shall have some occasion to speak of constitutions. We shall have no occasion to speak of treaties. We shall frequently have occasion to speak of statutes, and shall linger over eight famous statutes. We shall speak of rules and regulations of administrative bodies only once. It will be about the power of the Securities and Exchange Commission, commonly called the S.E.C., to lay down rules and regulations respecting the purchase of shares of stock on margin, — a topic of great practical importance with which we shall deal at length in discussing the modern law of pledge, — one of the outstanding topics of this course. But the bulk of our time, about two thirds of our time, will be devoted to the sixth kind of legal rules, — rules laid down by the courts in decisions.

Now, what influences courts in reaching their decisions? I must make some preliminary remarks:

First, as to the hierarchy of courts. Take England. For centuries there were three very important common-law courts, — the King's Bench, the Exchequer, and the Common Pleas. There were also various inferior courts. There were also courts of Chancery, the Admiralty Court, and other courts. The House of Lords, a judicial as well as a legislative body, was the court of last resort. Today the situation is roughly as follows: There are numerous inferior courts. Above them is the High Court, with various divisions, — there is the King's Bench Division, this division being the successor to the old King's Bench, the Exchequer, and the Common Pleas. There is also a Chancery Division, the successor to the old Chancery courts. There is also a Probate, Divorce, and Admiralty Division, the successor to various courts having jurisdiction in such matters. Above the High Court is the Court of Appeal. And above the Court of Appeal is the House of Lords. There is also the Judicial Committee of the

Privy Council, which deals with matters affecting colonies or dominions. The Judicial Committee of the Privy Council is, for example, the Canadian court of last resort. How long that will last is conjectural. In substance, Canada today is not a dominion, but a nation, and it would not surprise me to see it prefer to have a court of last resort the judges of which it appoints itself. But at present it is content to have the Judicial Committee of the Privy Council its court of last resort.

Now take the federal courts in this country. First come the District Courts, then the Circuit Courts of Appeals, and lastly the Supreme Court of the United States.

Take Massachusetts. There are various inferior courts, some of them disposing of a very large volume of litigation. The Municipal Court in Boston, for example, has each year tens of thousands of cases on its docket. Then comes the Superior Court. Then comes the Supreme Judicial Court. The correct title is not Supreme Court, but Supreme Judicial Court of Massachusetts.

Take New York. There are various inferior courts. Then comes what is called the Supreme Court. But then comes the Appellate Division, and then comes the Court of Appeals, so that the Supreme Court in New York is supreme only in name. It is analogous to the High Court in England.

If you are contemplating practice in any particular state, take a little time at once to familiarize yourself with the hierarchy of courts in your state. In no state is it more elaborate than the New York hierarchy, and in most states it is simpler.

And now a word as to the jurisdiction of the federal courts. A federal court may have jurisdiction because some federal question is involved, — some question under the United States Constitution, or under some treaty, or under some federal statute. Or it may have jurisdiction simply because the litigants are citizens of different states. A citizen of Massachusetts has, for example, a tort claim against a citizen of New York. No federal question is involved, but the proper federal court has jurisdiction to try it. This jurisdiction is not exclusive. If the plaintiff desires, he may bring his action in a state court, but, in such case, the defendant, if he desires, may usually remove it into a federal court.

Now, suppose that a question arises in some court, federal or state, which is not a court of last resort. The court will examine to see if there is any precedent *binding* upon it. That precise question may have been decided by some court higher in the hierarchy. Thus, if a question arises in the Superior Court of this state, and the Supreme Judicial Court has already decided that precise question, the judge will not re-examine it. He will automatically follow the decision of the Supreme Judicial Court. Similarly, if that precise question is a federal question, and the Supreme Court of the United States has decided it, he will likewise automatically follow its decision. But note this: A question may have been decided by the Supreme Court of the United States in a case where there was no federal question involved, but where the Court had jurisdiction only because of diversity of citizenship, and in such case the judge in the Superior Court of Massachusetts, although he will no doubt treat with great respect the decision of the Supreme Court of the United States, will not feel *bound* to follow it.

Is a court of last resort bound by its own previous decision of a question? In England, it is the received opinion that the House of Lords *is* bound by its own previous decision, — that it will never overrule itself. If the law is to be changed, there must be a statute. The House of Lords may, therefore, in its legislative capacity, concur in changing a rule which it has laid down in its judicial capacity, and which it refuses to change in its judicial capacity.

In this country, on the other hand, the Supreme Court of the United States has several times overruled itself. And I think it pretty safe to say that no state court of last resort would feel that it was necessarily *bound* to follow its own previous decision.

So much as to preliminary observations. But now suppose that a question arises in some court, federal or state, where the answer is not controlled either (1) by a constitutional provision, or (2) by a treaty, or (3) by a statute, or (4) by an ordinance or a rule or regulation of an administrative body, or (5) by a *binding* precedent. The court has, in such case, a free hand. *It has power to decide as it sees fit.* This is an immense power. A large part of our law is judge-made law. That fact should be neither smothered nor belittled, but frankly and fully recognized. There is a tale that once in a Massachusetts court a lawyer in the course of his argument spoke of a certain proposition as law. The judge intervened, saying: 'That is not the law.' The lawyer bowed and said: 'It *was* the law until your Honor spoke.'

On the Continent in Europe, the scope of the power of judges is less, definitely less, than in England or the United States.

That is because statutes cover most of the ground. But, even on the Continent in Europe, the statutes do not — cannot, in the nature of things — prescribe rules for every sort of question which may arise, and where the question is unanswered by any statute, the Continental judges also have a free hand. *In part*, even Continental law is judge-made law.

How should judges act in exercising power to lay down rules when they have a free hand? It is fundamental with us that we ought to have a government of laws and not of men. Therefore, a good judge will not decide a question until he has given due consideration to all relevant matters. What are those relevant matters? I will mention four:

1. *The pertinent facts.* The pertinent facts are *not* confined to the facts shown by the record. There may be other facts of which the court may, and should, take judicial notice. For example: In England, the tenant of land for life or years was not allowed to make many changes. To strip the land of timber was waste. But in this country stripping the land of timber was often the best way to develop the land. Another example: In early English law, an employer usually had only a few employees who knew each other and cooperated together. Today, an employer may have a very large number of employees and close cooperation may be impossible. Such changes in economic facts affecting the community which are matters of common knowledge ought to be given due consideration by the courts. A court will take judicial notice of what, as the phrase goes, 'everybody knows.'

2. *What other courts have done with respect to the same or similar questions.* And here carefully distinguish between (*a*) results reached, (*b*) reasons given, and (*c*) dicta dropped.

(*a*) *Results reached.* Lord Mansfield was born in Scotland, but he, like many another Scotsman, did very well for himself in London. For over thirty years he was Lord Chief Justice of England. A friend was appointed to a high administrative position overseas, and it was to be expected that in the exercise of his office he might on occasion be called upon to administer martial law. He was not a lawyer, and this part of his probable duties troubled him. He asked Mansfield's advice, and Mansfield said: 'Announce your decision, but give no reasons. Your good sense will probably enable you to reach, in at least most cases, a result which will be sensible and which will be so recognized. But if you give reasons, they will provoke discussion and might well be wrong.' Shrewd advice for such a situation.

'Oh,' you say, 'but that was martial law. Should it not be otherwise when there has been no resort to martial law?' Yes. Reasons should certainly be given in such case. A judge is not a good judge unless he gives his reasons. His decision should not be just an *ipse dixit*. But results, apart from reasons, are nevertheless important, have a good deal of persuasive value. Last year, I was much troubled about the right answer to a question which lay in the borderland between the law of property and the law of contract. I prepared a memorandum, stating the question, the result which I had tentatively reached, and my reasons for reaching that result, and submitted it to eight other persons in Langdell Hall. That made a court, so to speak, of nine, including myself. Seven of the nine reached my result. Of these seven, only one besides myself supported my result on my reasoning. Analysis showed that the seven had reached the result by four different lines of reasoning. I was far from being content with that, but at least took some comfort out of the fact that seven of nine reached the *result*. I felt pretty safe in concluding that the result at least was right. I repeat that results reached have considerable persuasive value.

(*b*) *Reasons given.* Sometimes the court will be unanimous as to the result reached and will give only one line of reasoning to justify that result. But not infrequently a court will announce two or more lines of reasoning. 'We decide for the plaintiff because &c. And, even if the plaintiff is not entitled to win on that ground, he is entitled to win because &c.' Alternative lines of reasoning have some tendency to weaken each other. And sometimes judges will file what are called concurring opinions. Concurring opinions, even more than alternative lines of reasoning acceptable to all members of the court, have some tendency to weaken each other.

(*c*) *Dicta dropped.* These are remarks which a judge drops which are not part of the *ratio decidendi*. An excellent judge, the legend runs, directed that the epitaph on his tombstone should consist solely of the words: 'He never made a dictum and he never regarded one.' May he rest in peace! Perhaps there may be exceptional cases where a dictum serves a useful purpose, but ordinarily at least dicta should not be made. Cut out the conversation, stick to the issue actually presented. When you are arguing, be shy of quoting dicta, and, if you do quote them, frankly recognize that they are *only* dicta, and therefore entitled to but little weight. And, if your adversary gives you an opening by quoting a dictum as though it was part of the *ratio decidendi*, pounce on him.

This applies not only to the arguments which you will make in actual practice, but also to the arguments which you will make in the law club work. Inability so to analyze an opinion as to distinguish dicta from reasoning is a badge of inadequacy.

I divert to recommend each one of you to join a law club, and take your law club work seriously, devoting about a quarter of your time to it, so long as the law club season lasts. It is a very valuable supplement to your regular work and will give you something which we cannot give you in the class.

Now, I have spoken of the results reached, the reasons given, and the dicta dropped by other courts. *What* other courts?

First will come courts in the same jurisdiction. Then courts in other states, preferably but not necessarily courts of last resort, and federal courts on questions other than federal questions.

Should you go even farther, and look at what courts in other countries have done? Yes. That is particularly true of English courts on matters which involve rules laid down long ago.

What was the law in the thirteen states immediately after the Revolution? By far the largest part of the law in each of those states was like the law in England at that time. To some small extent a particular colony may have already developed its own law through legislation by authorized legislative bodies, and/or decisions by authorized courts. But in the main the law consisted of English common law and English statutes. Now we said good-bye to stubborn, stupid, sanity-lacking George III, but there was no disposition to say good-bye to English common law, and to substitute in its place the French or any other system of law. There were many reasons for that. The colonists were well satisfied with English law. Indeed, they considered that they were fighting for English law, — that the rule that there should be no taxation without representation was a rule of English law. It was not English law, but the flouting of English law by an English sovereign to which they objected. They prized English law as part of their heritage. Moreover, business men were accustomed to doing business on the basis of English law and they had no desire to change. Besides, a cynic may observe, most judges and lawyers knew no other law, and would naturally seek to preserve the value of what they did know. I have never run across in any American history any evidence that any responsible person ever suggested that either our private law or our criminal law should be based on anything other than English law.

Now, quite frequently questions will arise which cannot be answered without tracing the development of English law. In no branch of the law does that occur more often than in the law of property, and a considerable number of the cases which we shall discuss are English cases. These cases are not confined to cases decided before 1776, for developments of English law in England after 1776 often have persuasive value. And decisions in other countries, notably Canada, on matters stemming back to early English law are often of persuasive value.

Shall we go still farther and examine the decisions in those countries, like Italy, Germany, France, Spain, where the modern law largely stems from the old Roman law? In the thirteen original states and in all other states which are within the bounds of the United States, as defined in the Treaty of 1783, the law is chiefly based upon English law. But the original territory of the United States is only about a quarter of its present territory. A large part of our territory was acquired by the Louisiana Purchase, and here the law was at the time based on French law. The law in Texas was originally based on Spanish law, and that remark also applies to those parts of our territory which have been acquired from Spain or Mexico by purchase or conquest. To some extent, in many states, there are still at least traces of French or Spanish law. In Louisiana there is much more than traces of French law. Louisiana decided to base its criminal law on English law, but its private law is still based to a very large extent on French law, although there has been a considerable infiltration of English law. In Texas, California, and other states there are still important traces of Spanish law. I shall have occasion to speak of this again when I mention community property, a method of holding property known to both the French law and the Spanish law, but unknown to the common law. But it is safe to make the generalization that viewing the country as a whole it is rare that a question arises where a court would feel it was likely to derive much assistance by examining the decisions of any modern country where the law is not based on the common law.

How about Roman law? That was the product of a highly developed civilization, enriched by contributions from many minds of the first order. Some of the very early writers in England sought to introduce Roman law, and to some extent they succeeded. You will, for example, find references to Roman law in some topics discussed in this course, and its study has affected the thinking of some eminent jurists, including Story, a justice of the Supreme Court of the United States, who was the first professor in this Law School. But I do not think that the influence of Roman law has been very large upon American law, and today only occasionally would an advocate increase his chances of persuading the court by citing authorities from the Roman law.

3. So much for the results reached, the reasons given, and the dicta dropped by other courts. We pass from this to the third of the matters which influence judges, — the writings of jurists (who may or may not be judges). A person gives his opinion as to what the law was, or is, or ought to be. How persuasive is that with courts? It, of course, depends on the person who is giving the opinion, — a court may treat such opinion with great respect, or it may dismiss it with irritation.

I will speak of five famous writers: I begin with Littleton who wrote on *Tenures*. Littleton was one of the King's justices, and served for many years. In those days there was not much law except land law and criminal law. Probably most of the cases which Littleton was called upon to decide, outside of criminal cases, were land-law cases. He was therefore well qualified to write on land law. The treatise is a short one and the literary style is good. It is commonly accepted as an accurate statement of the law on tenures as it stood in 1481, the first date I ask you to remark.

Then comes Coke's *Commentaries* on Littleton. Coke was Speaker of the House of Commons in the days of Elizabeth when the Speaker was, in substance, Tribune of the People. He did not, on occasion, hesitate to oppose Elizabeth. But she justified the Salic law by recognizing his worth and made him her Attorney-General. Later, he was made Chief Justice of the Court of Common Pleas, and later Chief Justice of the King's Bench, as such being Lord Chief Justice of England. He stood up to James I, when James sought to enlarge the royal prerogative. A question involving this was likely to come before Coke. James had him sounded, — would he not assure His Majesty that the decision would be favorable to prerogative? Coke's reply deserves to be immortal. He said that when such a question came before him he would endeavor to decide it as in reason and right it ought to be decided. His opposition to James finally landed him in the Tower, but he never became subservient. He was the Tribune of the Judiciary.

Coke's writings include his reports of many cases. These are frequently cited simply *Reports*, without any name. They are *the* Reports. Then he also wrote his *Institutes*, and the first of these was his *Commentaries* on Littleton, for which the correct citation is *Co. Litt.* The first edition was published in 1628, the second date I ask you to remember. The *Commentaries* are much longer than the *Tenures* of Littleton upon which he is commenting. He will take a section of Littleton of a few lines, and his comments may extend to several pages. Mansfield called Coke an uncouth and crabbed author, and no doubt there are one or more headaches in almost every page. But the *Commentaries* show a wealth of learning, and a massive and dynamic intellect. Coke, through his *Reports* and *Institutes*, has had, I think, a greater influence upon the common law than any other man dead or living. Three centuries have flashed by since Coke wrote, and I think many of the things he said *ought* not to be *any longer* law. But I think he is entitled to ride at the head of the common-law procession, — complete with plume, and penetrating eye, and rapier tongue, and juristic thunderbolts poised in either hand.

To divert on a question of pronunciation. Coke pronounced his name Cook. His descendants now living all call themselves Cook. But in this country most judges have pronounced, and still pronounce, his name Coke. It is rather puzzling to know how to speak of him. Dean Pound says that you ought to pronounce his name as he himself pronounced it, so he is Cook to Dean Pound. But I think it is preferable to pronounce his name as it has been commonly pronounced by judges in this country, and so I speak of him to you as Coke. I say (or try to say) Pa-ree when I am in France, but I say Paris when I am in America. But the question of pronunciation is not worth disputing about.

The next treatise-writer that ought to be mentioned is Blackstone. He was the first professor of the common law at Oxford, and his *Commentaries* are in substance lectures which were delivered there. The publication was completed shortly before the American Revolution. Blackstone was later made a judge. The literary quality of the *Commentaries* is good. A readable exposition of the English law, written just before the Revolution by a person of high standing, was naturally much used in this country. Blackstone's *Commentaries* were for more than a century the outstanding textbook in America, and there are many states even at the present time where a person taking his bar examinations is

expected to know his Blackstone. But Blackstone did not have
the massive dynamic intellect that Coke had.

As to treatises written by Americans. Kent was a judge in
New York, — a learned, reliable, wise judge. In intellect I think
that he definitely surpassed Blackstone. His *Commentaries* were
written more than a century ago, but in tracing the development
of American law they are still of great value.

Story did not write a single work, as did Blackstone and Kent,
covering the whole field of law. But he wrote a large number of
treatises on various topics, and these have been received with
great respect by courts both in this country and in England.

If sometime you will look at the names carved on the outside
of this building, — Story, Greenleaf, Parsons, Washburn, Thayer,
Gray, Smith, Ames, — you will see the names of eight members
of the Faculty, the writings of every one of whom have been
received with respect by courts, and have influenced decisions.
The like remark may be made of Langdell, the first Dean of this
School, after whom this building was named.

We will begin tomorrow with the discussion of *Pierson* v. *Post*,
and *Keeble* v. *Hickeringill*.

A LECTURE IN PROPERTY I
GIVEN TOWARD THE CLOSE OF THE YEAR ON
THE STATUTE OF USES

WE HAVE now climbed to a mental height from which it is possible to get a good view of the whole Valley of the Statute of
Uses.

Two things stand out. One is that the Statute failed to accomplish its main purpose. The other is that, nevertheless, it
produced two important by-products: (1) new methods of conveyancing, and (2) new legal future interests.

When the bill was before Parliament the cry was, 'Down
with the Uses.' It has been said that probably at least half the
land in England was at that time held by feoffees to uses. There
was a widespread dual ownership of land, — an equitable ownership on top of a legal ownership. The purpose of the Statute
was to end such dual ownership.

Now, suppose that T was at that time seised in fee to the use
of C in fee. This existing dual ownership *might* have been ended

by eliminating C, — by enacting that T should hold free of any use. It could have been done, but it would have been shocking to do it. In substance it would have been taking one man's property and giving it to another. Therefore, the legislature enacted that T, not C, should be eliminated, and that, although C's equitable fee was destroyed, he should be given in its place a like legal fee. *What C had had in equity he was thereafter to have at law.*

So much as to existing uses. But how about future uses? In Louisiana today [this lecture was given before 1938], if B agrees to hold land to the use of C, C takes nothing. There is a public policy against dual ownership. An attempt to create a use is abortive, — void *ab initio*. The English legislature *might* have taken the Louisiana way. You will never understand the significance of the Statute until you see clearly that the English legislature did *not* take the Louisiana way. I conjecture — of course, it is only a conjecture — that the draftsmen of the Statute thought that they would be doing a more neat, masterly piece of draftsmanship if they killed two birds with one stone and disposed of both existing and future uses by one formula. Therefore, instead of providing that an attempt thereafter to create a use should be void *ab initio*, they proceeded on the assumption that no obstacle whatever should be placed upon the further creation of uses, and contented themselves with providing that the very instant an equitable estate was created, it should be changed into a like legal estate. It was as though the Lord when He created man should have seen fit first to create an angel and instantly to translate that angel into Adam.

This was reaching the desired result by a roundabout way. Why did the Statute fail to end the dual ownership of land, even in this roundabout way? The answer is that, in three respects, the courts gave a narrow, restrictive construction to the Statute.

(1) The Statute applied only to a person who was 'seised' to the use of another. 'Seised' was good Plantagenet for 'possessed,' but a new meaning was arising under which 'seised' connoted a freehold estate. The Statute was construed as using 'seised' in this new sense. Therefore B, having a fee, might convey to T a term for ten thousand years (there was no common-law limit to the length of a term of years) to the use of C and others, and such case would not be within the scope of the Statute.

(2) The Statute was construed to apply only to what are

commonly called 'passive' uses. If B enfeoffed T to the use of C, and imposed duties upon T, the performance of which required T to retain the legal title, the case was held not to be within the scope of the Statute. Thus, if T is to collect the rents and profits and apply the net rents and profits for the benefit of, or pay them over to, C for life. Thus, too, at least according to *Ayer* v. *Ritter*, if, on the death of C, T is 'to convey to D.' You will hear more of this case next year.

(3) The Statute was construed to apply only to a T who acquired seisin by force of the common law. In *Tyrrel's Case*, B bargained and sold (the deed being duly enrolled) to T, to the use of C and others. A bargain and sale is a promise to hold land to the use of another (enforcible because made for a consideration). Therefore, B (first story) had agreed to hold land to the use of T (second story) to the use of C (third story). This was a young skyscraper, and violated building restrictions. The courts did the Louisiana to the third story. C took nothing, either at law or in equity. 'An use cannot be engendered of a use.'

This was plainly unjust. T, the fiduciary, was enriched at the expense of those whom B had intended should be the beneficiaries. The courts later repented, and refused to follow *Tyrrel's Case*. In like later cases, T was obliged to hold the land for the benefit of C. Therefore, T was seised to the use of C. When the courts to this extent corrected the error of *Tyrrel's Case*, why did they not take the logical second step and hold that C's equitable estate was by the Statute changed into a like legal estate? Such a case would certainly seem to be within the words of the Statute. I think that no really satisfactory answer to this question has ever been given. The fashionable answer is that the Statute was intended to apply only to a person who became seised by operation of the Statute itself. This answer leaves me with eyebrows up. I think that the courts failed to recognize frankly the full extent of the error in *Tyrrel's Case*. It was like a shortstop who fumbles a double-play grounder and only half retrieves his fumble by getting the ball to first in time. In any event, for some good reason or for no good reason, the law was settled that if B bargained and sold to T to the use of C, then, although (1) T had a freehold estate, and although (2) the use was 'passive,' nevertheless C's estate was only an equitable estate.

By those three constructions, the Statute shrank, and shrank, and shrank. The Statute failed to end the dual ownership of land. In that part of the Valley of the Statute of Uses, nothing meets the eye except ruins, interesting for historical reasons.

But the Statute did produce two important by-products. The first of these by-products was the new methods of conveyancing, — the bargain and sale, and the covenant to stand seised.

Now, in the Plantagenet days possession loomed very large indeed. It is not, therefore, surprising to find that in Plantagenet days a present freehold estate could not be created or transferred except by livery of seisin, — that is to say, by delivery of the possession of the land itself. Now, if B had a fee and wished to convey a fee to C, it might well be inconvenient for B and C to go to the land. There was a growing demand from laymen for a new method of conveyancing by which land could be conveyed by a delivery of a deed, instead of the delivery of the land itself. The draftsmen of the Statute of Uses and of the Statute of Enrolments (passed at or about the same time) intended to meet this demand, and also to pick up some revenue by permitting land to be conveyed by an enrolled bargain and sale. But they carelessly drafted the Statute of Enrolments so that it only applied where the bargain and sale was of a freehold estate. This led to the use of the conveyancing tandem which was for centuries so popular in England, — the leader being the colt, 'Term of Years' (by Statute of Uses out of Equity), and the wheel-horse being good old 'Commonlaw Release.'

In the United States the Statute of Uses was, forthwith after the Revolution, in force in all states, and it is still in force in most of the states. The Statute of Enrolments has never been in force in any state. Therefore, if B, having a fee, wished to convey a fee to C, all he had to do was to deliver to C a deed of bargain and sale, and I believe that more acres of land in the United States have been conveyed by that method than by all other methods of conveyance combined. And that part of the Valley of the Statute of Uses is still productive. It is not producing such large crops as it once did, because legislatures have introduced local statutory methods of conveyances which compete, and sometimes wholly supplant. But it has produced very large crops and still produces substantial crops.

The second by-product of the Statute of Uses was of even greater importance. The common law had had the rigid rules about the creation of future estates or interests which we have inventoried. Equity declined to follow that rigidity. The common law was simple, but rigid; equity was complicated, but it did heed the intent of the grantors by permitting shifting and springing uses. And now see, and see clearly, the outstanding principle: *The liberality of equity as to the creation of future interests was (at least usually) by the Statute of Uses carried over into the law, so that new kinds of legal future interests became permissible.* That is the most important single sentence in all that I have said to you about the Statute of Uses. Ponder it.

That part of the Valley of the Statute of Uses which is devoted to the production of new kinds of legal future interests is the most prosperous part of the Valley today. The demand for these new legal future interests is increasing rather than decreasing. The lawyer who can produce reliable and artistic future interests is likely to be in demand. Many of you will want to equip yourselves to draw complicated trust settlements and complicated wills, replete with future interests. If so, you should go on into the course in Future Interests and there study problems of great intellectual difficulty and great practical importance.

On some matters I follow the lead of Coke, or Mansfield, or Eldon. On some, the lead of Kent or Story. But lately I have been following the lead of Moses. I have given you the twelve Tables of the Law of Conveyancing, and now I bring you within sight, but only within sight, of the Promised Land of Future Interests, a land flowing with intellectual milk and financial honey. It will be for others to guide you in the Promised Land.

Chapter Six

MISCELLANY

AN AFTER–DINNER SPEECH

THE Illinois Bar Association gave a dinner at Chicago on December 29, 1915, in honor of the Association of American Law Schools. The speech given below was one of those given after that dinner. It was published by the *Illinois Law Review*, in its issue of February, 1916, under the caption 'The Welter of Decisions.'

In the preface to the third part of his *Reports*, Sir Edward Coke said that the kings of the realm had, in former times, appointed four professors of law, learned and discreet, to report the judgments and opinions of the reverend judges,

> To the end that all the judges and justices in all the several parts of the realm might, as it were with one mouth in all men's cases, pronounce one and the same sentence; whose learned works are extant and digested into nine several volumes wherein you may observe the unity and consent of so many several judges and courts in so many successions of ages and the coherence and concordance of such infinite, several and divers cases (one, as it were, with sweet consent and amity, proving and approving another).

And then he proceeded to enumerate other estimable law books, such as Glanville, Bracton, and Littleton, the *Commentaries* of Plowden, the *Abridgements* of Fitzherbert and Brooke, and his 'own simple labours.' And he sums up by saying:

> Then have you fifteen books or treatises and as many volumes of the reports besides the abridgements of the common law.

There has been a controversy as to whether the kings of the realm ever did appoint those four professors of the law, learned and discreet, to report the judges, but I think no one has ever questioned the completeness of the review by Coke of the books on the common law then existing. And the total of those books was about thirty.

In recent years numerous gentlemen have called the attention of the public to the rapid multiplication of new legal products. The work of a court today has been compared with the work of a court a century ago; the number of reported decisions has been contrasted with the number a generation, or some years, past. I wish to speak of the matter not relatively, but absolutely.

How many pages do you suppose are contained in the reports of the decisions of courts in the United States which appear within a single year? We took the volumes of such reports which were added to the library of the Harvard Law School in the year ending June 30, 1915, and ascertained with substantial accuracy the number of pages contained therein; we excluded all reports in the nature of duplicates, — for example, with some relatively unimportant exceptions, we excluded such reports as the *Atlantic Reporter* and the *Northeastern Reporter*. We then did the same thing with regard to the reports of the English decisions. The total number of pages in the English reports for a year was about five thousand; the total number of pages in the American reports for a year was about one hundred and seventy-five thousand.

Now, if anybody can be expected to keep up with the new legal products, I take it that a professor at a law school is that one. Suppose a professor takes six weeks in the year real vacation, and that the correction of his examination books at the end of the year takes him into the wilderness for six weeks. This leaves him with forty weeks, and we will assume that he works eight hours a day. Now he will be lucky if, after he has done his other duties at the law school, he has left free for study twenty-four hours a week, — the equivalent of three full days. If a professor did no writing and no thinking, but simply read reports all the time, he would have to develop and maintain a speed of a hundred and eighty pages an hour, just to read the annual outpouring. And that takes no account of a variety of other things on which he would like to keep himself informed, and on which he ought to keep himself informed. Thus, of the decisions in other countries, notably England, but also the Continental countries; the vast amount of statutes which are appearing; the reports of the commissions, — there is scarcely anything that is much more important than what the Interstate Commerce Commission is doing; and lastly, the treatises and articles which appear on legal subjects.

Viewing the matter not relatively but absolutely, it is plain that the time is past when a man can, by putting out a little more, and yet a little more, of his energy, keep up with the annual outpouring. The mass of the annual legal products is so great that it will break the back of any man who tries to carry it. However conscientious he may be, in self-preservation he simply must stand out from under.

It is easy to state a difficulty; it is hard to suggest a remedy. In those immortal words of Tweed: 'What are you going to do about it?'

The obvious suggestion to be made first is that of specialization. Now specialization may be of two kinds. A man may confine himself to a few subjects or to one subject. A man may confine himself to a few jurisdictions or to one jurisdiction.

First, as to a specialization in subjects. It is now almost the universal practice in American law schools that a professor should offer the same courses indefinitely, or at least over a long period of time. Experience shows that that gives the best results for the students, so long, at least, as the professor keeps his intellectual conscience. The elder Thayer was fond of saying that good teaching came when the teacher was guiding his students over a road oft-traveled by himself; and that, of course, means specialization. But the professor who is most proficient in any given subject is constantly striving to show to his students that the law is, or should be, a harmonious whole; that it is not split up into thought-tight compartments. And he is constantly striving to help his students to develop a capacity for legal judgment by encouraging them to reason by analogy from other topics in the law. To keep himself at a high efficiency, he must keep himself informed as to what is happening in other subjects than those he is teaching. Moreover, even if you assume that a professor could safely confine himself to one quarter of the decisions, and if you assume (what would probably not be true) that he could safely delegate to some assistant the selection of that quarter, the figures already given will show that while, perhaps, he could make his eye travel over one quarter of the annual production, he could not possibly digest it. And when we come to consider the judges, it is plain that a specialization in subjects will not solve the difficulty. They cannot specialize in subjects. It is a part of their job to be such all-around persons that they are equally at ease in considering a restraint on the alienation of property, and a lack of restraint in the alienation of affections.

Second, as to a specialization in jurisdictions. This morning, at one of the meetings of the Association of Law Schools, Mr. Kales called our attention to the fact that there is no common law in the United States; that we have no final court except on federal questions; but instead, he said, there was a common law in each of forty-seven jurisdictions. He went on to develop his topic until he showed, or asserted, that there was a common law for each law school, and finally that there was a common law for each law professor.

'Common law.' What does 'common' mean? I submit that a thing is only common when it is shared by many, and the logical outcome of Mr. Kales's definition would seem to be that he has a common law which he shares with nobody. Of course, it is true that we do not have in this country any court corresponding to the House of Lords, but does that mean that we cannot have a common law in America? On all things it is not to be expected that the law will be the same or even substantially the same. There is no reason why the law of water rights in Colorado should be the same as the law of water rights in Massachusetts, — the reason is the other way, there should be a difference. I suppose that if we should take this body of men and go through it, we could not possibly find any two men who think the same on all legal points. But does that mean that we do not have certain fundamental conceptions in common? Not at all.

Now, up to the present time it has certainly been the custom of American courts, when they were confronted with some new problem, not to attempt to solve that out of their own inner consciousness, but to look to the decisions in other jurisdictions for information, suggestion, guidance. And the result has usually been that a court, finding a certain trend of authority in the United States, has been glad to conform to that, and has only with regret departed from it if local conditions seemed to make that necessary. Now, to my mind, that is a common law more splendid than the common law which depends upon the decisions of the House of Lords. It is one thing to have all courts following a rule because that rule is imposed upon them by a higher court, — but how much greater weight does it carry when you find that court after court in the United States has been presented with a problem and they have felt that they could come to the same decision, — the decision not being imposed upon them by some higher court, but being adopted by them in respect to the decisions in other jurisdictions. If we continue with this enormous mass of decisions it may become impossible for a court to take that attitude of carefully considering cases outside the jurisdiction.

We are living in a time when it is plain that the American people need to strengthen every force that tends to bind them together and quicken their consciousness of themselves, as parts of one nation. Just as we want a common language, so, it seems to me, we greatly want a common law, in the sense in which I have spoken of it. For the courts of any one jurisdiction to confine themselves to cases in their own jurisdiction is, to be sure, one sort of solution. But it seems to me that it is the kind of solution to be likened to the throwing overboard of the cargo when the ship is in distress.

I conclude that there is no satisfactory solution out of the difficulty in which we are through either sort of specialization.

The affirmative suggestions which I offer are four.

First: Let the court write no opinion, or, at most, a mere memorandum opinion, in the cases which do not deserve an extended opinion.

A few years ago one of the justices of the Supreme Judicial Court of Massachusetts told me that there was no real merit in three quarters of the cases that came before that court. And yet that court goes on today writing an extended opinion in practically every case. There are very few cases that really add anything to the law; most of them are merely cumulative, at best. For a court to write an extended opinion to gratify the vanity of counsel in every case, but to direct that only a few be officially reported, would not meet the difficulty, for we should forthwith have in our midst some enterprising publisher who would bring out the unofficial reports.

I turn once more to Coke. After his enumeration of the books he proceeds to say:

> In troth, if judges should set down the reasons and causes of their judgments within every record, that immense labor should withdraw them from the necessary services of the commonwealth and their records should grow to be like *elephantini libri*, of infinite length, and in mine opinion lose somewhat of their present authority and reverence; and this is also worthy for learned and grave men to imitate.

Coke, with thirty volumes on the law, warning the judges not
to report all their decisions!

The Court of Appeals of New York has set the country a
splendid example which, I think, is not at present appreciated.
Turn to the last volume, 215, of the records of the New York
Court of Appeals; you will find that, excluding such things as
motions for reargument, the court disposed of 202 cases. Of
those, 157 were disposed of with no opinion, or with mere memorandum opinions. In only 63, or 28 per cent of the whole, did
the court write an extended opinion.

Second: Let the judges be required to write their own headnotes.

It was my first thought to bring here and to read as horrible
examples some of the headnotes which have appeared in recent
volumes. I have not done so because the cases might be identi-
fied and the personality of the reporter revealed. But I submit
that frequently it is literally harder to read and understand the
headnote than it is to read and understand the opinion. In a
great many cases it seems to me the fault is not wholly, or even
primarily, with the reporter. There is many an opinion which
reads as if the judge had been having a real comfortable chat
with his stenographer. I have devoted myself to such cases in a
conscientious mood until I have revolted. The reading of decision after decision of that kind does not increase a man's brain
power, — it actually deteriorates his mentality. It produces
nothing but brain fag and brain fog.

It is the perfection of knowledge to be able to say true things
in a few words. It is only when the judge is confused in his own
mind that he cannot even sum up concisely. My first suggestion
would buttress my second. If the judges wrote fewer opinions
they could write better opinions.

The requirement that the judge should write his own headnotes, that he should be able to state in a few words what is the
point of what he is talking about, would not only save us from
the work of inadequate reporters, but it would tend to save us
from a mass of decisions in which no one can see wisdom except
by a most benevolent inference.

Third: The lawyers can help by confining their citations to a
few pertinent cases or, at most, by sharply differentiating between the most pertinent cases and those which are merely
cumulative. And while the lawyers may be a bit timid about
doing that, yet I feel sure that they will not prejudice the cause

of their clients by so doing. Not long ago a lawyer was arguing before a court in an eastern jurisdiction and he said: 'Your Honors will find that, beginning at page so and so of my brief, and continuing thereon, I have collected all of the authorities on this point.' The presiding judge leaned forward and said: 'Did you put the best one at the top?'

A great mass of decisions does not aid the judge, it simply swamps him. And the judges are going to be more favorable to the men who present their cases in the more condensed way.

Fourth: The professors ought to help some. Again avoiding all personalities, I submit that most of the law books that are now put out consist, so far as the text is concerned, of loose, general statements which, on analysis, are seen to be inconsistent with each other, to which are appended dense black clouds of notes. The idea seems to be that all that is necessary is to get in all the authorities. There is but one God and His name is All the Authorities. Those books show infinitely more industry than brains. The scissors are mightier than the pen.

It is good to be learned, but it is so much more important to have a little wisdom. The kinds of books which would be of great service and which, it seems to me, the professors really owe a duty to the community to produce, are books which will state the problems concisely, and then discuss those problems, with great respect for the authorities and in the light of the authorities, but also in the light of what seems reasonable to the writer. I want to predict that such books will be gladly welcomed by the courts as an aid to them in discharging their duty of keeping our law so simple that it can be understood, and so reasonable that it can be approved.

And one last word: I have spoken of the lawyers and I have spoken of the professors, but I wish to make it plain that I do not overestimate what either of them can do. The ultimate responsibility for keeping our law simple and reasonable must, under our conceptions, rest with the courts. The opinions which will command the respect of our people are those that are given with a full sense of official responsibility, with a consciousness that the judgment pronounced will have an actual effect on the human beings involved in the litigation.

A SOCRATIC DIALOGUE
BETWEEN W (THE AUTHOR) AND X (A JUNIOR COLLEAGUE)

From *Margin Customers*, pp. 98–107

W. For years I 'went along' with the traditional view that a promise to pay money, not evidenced by a negotiable instrument, is not assignable, — at least that it is not assignable at law. But now I question that. I do not see any valid reason why B, the legal owner of the right to receive a sum of money, should not be allowed to substitute C in his place as the *legal* owner of that right. Do you still adhere to the traditional view?

X. In a sense 'Yes,' but in a more important sense 'No.' You and I would probably reach the same results, but by different processes of reasoning. A makes a promise to B to pay a sum of money to B. I don't see how you can require A to pay that money to C without forcing on him a contract which he never made. Has not that thought given you pause?

W. Yes. Of course, there cannot be an enforcible promise without a promisee, and therefore if A makes an enforcible promise to B, to pay a sum of money to B, B is indispensable to the creation of the contract right. But once the contract right has been created, I do not, after reflection, have any difficulty in thinking of B simply as owner of the contract right so created. Now, marketability is a usual and desirable incident of ownership. Business men desire to be able to market *all* debts owned by them, if they have a business reason therefor. Therefore, I should like B to have the right to substitute C in his place as the legal owner of any contract right to receive payment of a sum of money, and I see nothing in the nature of a contract which blocks this.

X. I wish I could persuade myself to take, as easily as you do, the thought of eliminating the personality of B from the contract. I can't help feeling that B's personality is connected with the contract right, even *after* it is created. You concede that it was a promise to B to pay a sum of money *to B*?

W. Yes. But you underline *to B* in your thought, while I underline '*to pay a sum of money*' in my thought. I lay emphasis on the nature of the act to be done. I inquire whether it does, or does not, involve what would popularly be called a 'personal' relationship. There is a difference in kind and not merely in degree between a promise to marry B, where, of course, B's personality should never be eliminated, and a promise to pay a sum of money to B.

X. Perhaps that underlining does express the difference between us.

W. Would it be fair to say that you think of B and the contract right as Siamese twins?

X. I wince at the cartoon. But I cannot fairly object to it as a cartoon.

W. If B died, would the contract right die?

X. No. But that does not trouble me, for the executor or administrator is viewed as continuing B's personality.

W. If B went bankrupt, would you have any difficulty in allowing his trustee in bankruptcy to succeed to the ownership of the contract right?

X. No. But the trustee would take because the bankruptcy statute so directed.

W. You would not, however, denounce that statute as making a provision which ought not to have been made?

X. No. I have no difficulty about a succession in the ownership produced by operation of law. But I think the connection between the personality of B and the contract right ought not to be severed by the voluntary act of B.

W. You think that C may, by the voluntary act of B, be substituted for B as the person who has the right to receive the money from A, *only* if there is a novation?

X. Only if there is a novation. But where A makes a promise to pay to the *order* of B, he consents in advance to a novation.

W. Do you object to B's substituting C as the legal owner of a debt not evidenced by a negotiable instrument as being unfair to A?

X. Is the debt to be assignable, or negotiable?

W. Assignable only. I want C to be in no better position than that in which B was when he ceased to be owner; I want C to have derivative rights only.

X. Then I see no unfairness to A. The case is well within section 151 of the Restatement, Contracts, which seems sound to me.

W. When that section speaks of assignability, do you construe it to mean assignability in law or assignability in equity?

X. Assignability in law.

W. I have some difficulty in reconciling that construction of section 151 of the Restatement with section 447 of Williston's treatise on *Contracts*.

X. I do not think you should seek to reconcile them. In his treatise, Williston is giving us the benefit of his own convictions, opinions, and conclusions. But the Restatement is a composite product. The restaters, as I understand it, sought to agree as to the *results*. They were concerned to state results reached, where they were in agreement as to results, without specifying whether these results were reached by travelling by the equitable road *or* by the legal road. I have reason to believe that Williston thought that the rights, and the limitations of the rights, of the assignee so stated were those established by courts of equity, with the sole exception made by section 174 where he, as Reporter, accepted the views of his advisers as to the road to be travelled. He accepted that, as worded, because he himself thought that the result might perhaps be the better result, from the practical point of view, even if it was not logically consistent with travelling by the equitable road.

There were, I have been informed, some differences of opinion, and, if there was to be a Restatement, there had to be more or less give and take. Sole responsibility or credit for the Restatement should, therefore, not be placed upon, or given to, Williston. The treatise is Williston, pure and simple. But the Restatement is the product of a group. If the treatise and the Restatement are not altogether harmonious, that is not due to any confused thinking by Williston.

W. The Restatement is Williston, *plus?*

X. Or Williston, *minus*, as the case may be.

W. Do you use 'assignable' and 'transferable' as interchangeable terms?

X. (After a pause.) That is the most searching question you have asked. My impulse was to answer 'Yes,' but, after reflection, I answer 'No.' Transferability connotes to my mind the transfer of the legal title. Assignability does not connote that to my mind. I now think of it as a more comprehensive term than transferability. I should think it might well be used to cover both (*a*) cases where the legal title is transferred, and also (*b*) cases where through the giving of a legal power the same results are produced *as though* the legal title had been transferred.

W. But you do not think that a book debt is assignable in equity only?

X. No. Using assignable, as under the influence of your question I now define it, I have no difficulty in saying that the book debt is assignable at law.

W. Will you spell out for me your thoughts as to the assignability of contract rights for the payment of money, when not evidenced by negotiable instruments?

X. I think in terms of legal *power*, rather than legal *title*. I think that B can give C a power to collect the debt from A.

W. A legal power?

X. Yes.

W. Some have said that B gives C a beneficial agency. Do you distinguish between a power and a beneficial agency?

X. Definitely, yes. I regard a beneficial agency as a legal monstrosity. An agent is one who acts for another. A beneficial agency is a contradiction in terms.

W. So you would join me in throwing beneficial agency out of the window?

X. I would do more than that. I would open the window.

W. At least one of our colleagues thinks that B, after assignment to C, should be regarded as in the same position as he would be in if he had declared himself trustee of the debt for C. Does that appeal to you?

X. It once did. The idea has its attractions.

W. But not now for you?

X. No. It long ago receded into the background of my mind.

W. Have you thrown it out of the back window?

X. I haven't been quite as rough as that with it.

W. Any danger of your returning to an old love?

X. No.

W. Do you think that the two ideas of legal power and a quasi-declaration of trust are compatible?

X. No. I have talked with people who had one foot on the back of legal power and one foot on the back of quasi-declaration of trust. It is dangerous riding and I do not attempt the feat.

W. Do you under the doctrine of legal power always reach the same results as I reach under the doctrine of legal title?

X. Yes.

W. Always?

X. Yes. That is a searching question, but I have carefully thought it out.

W. You give the bona fide purchaser of a power just as great rights and just as full protection, even against persons who have

acquired some equitable right in the debt, as you would give to
a bona fide purchaser of the legal title?

X. Yes.

W. Take a pledge case which is worrying me. A incurs a debt
to B. It is not evidenced by any document, but B required A
to pledge certain articles with him before he would extend credit.
Let us say that a ship chandler, B, requires the captain of a ship,
A, to deposit security before he will supply the ship. B then sells
the security to D, a bona fide purchaser. Would you agree that
B became constructive trustee of the debt for the benefit of D?

X. Certainly.

W. Now, suppose that thereafter B makes to C, another bona
fide purchaser, an assignment of the debt. Who is the person
entitled to receive payment of that debt from A?

X. C.

W. Hurrah! That is for me the question, *par excellence*, and
that is the answer I hoped for.

X. That is the result given by section 174 of the Restatement,
which seems to me sound. But that should be read side by side
with section 167, and due consideration should be given to *both*
sections.

W. I am familiar with both sections and wholeheartedly
agree. The question I put to you fairly presents the issue between legal assignability and equitable assignability. D acquired an equity in the debt. If C acquired only an equity, his
equity would be a second equity, and, therefore, presumably
the inferior equity. But if C acquired the legal title, then, as he
is a bona fide purchaser, he would take that legal title free from
fourth-party equities. Now, I understand you to hold that a
bona fide purchaser of a legal power takes that free from fourth-
party equities.

X. I am not familiar with the expression 'fourth-party
equity.'

W. In any case relating to the assignment of a debt there are
necessarily three parties, — A, the debtor; B, the creditor; and
C, the assignee. But a fourth party *may* be in the picture. In
this case D is that fourth party.

X. I see. You use 'fourth-party' equity where I speak of an
'affirmative' equity. I now understand. You correctly state
my position. My mind moves quickly to the conclusion that C
takes free of D's equity.

W. Williston has a deep-rooted conviction that when A makes

an enforcible promise to B to pay a sum of money to B, the personality of B is built into the very structure of the contract, and that this conception should be respected except in cases where courts of equity have held that adhering to this conception would cause fraud on a third party, and where it is also true that failure to adhere will cause no substantial injury to either of the original parties.

He thinks that courts of equity have held, and rightly held, that, after the debtor has notice of the assignment, he should not be allowed to disregard every fact other than the personal relationship between debtor and creditor, and, therefore, that he should not be allowed to pay the original creditor, regardless of what is fair between that creditor and a third party who has come into the picture.

Unquestionably, his view is the traditional view in the common law, and it also receives sanction from the Roman law. Do you share his convictions?

X. Yes. At least I have those convictions. I really derived them from his teachings, and am unable to uproot them from my mind.

W. Williston has no difficulty in, say, ninety per cent of the cases with what, if 'transferability' is used as a term connoting the passing of the legal title, may be called the substantive, or business, results of transferability?

X. None at all.

W. But he thinks that sometimes, say, in ten per cent of the cases, legal transferability produces an inequitable result, and he wants equity to be the master, using legal machinery only as a servant.

X. I do not think that you read his mind correctly.

W. You surprise me. How do you read his mind?

X. He goes deeper than that. Transferability results do not, even in ten per cent of the cases, disturb him as inequitable; they disturb him as being opposed to the best interests of the business community. He is fully as eager to meet the needs of business men as you and I are.

W. You say that transferability results do not, even in ten per cent of the cases, disturb him as inequitable. Will you spell that out for me?

X. If there is one rascal, and one bona fide purchaser, it is inequitable that the rascal should win. But if there is one rascal and two bona fide purchasers, that is another matter. If you

have two bona fide purchasers, C and D, and the rascal has involved them, it is not inequitable that C should prevail over D,
but equally it is not inequitable that D should prevail over C.
There is nothing which shocks the conscience in either result.
It is just too bad that one of them has to lose, but in such cases
that is inevitable.

W. Unless the court splits it, giving some part to C, and some
part to D. I have read somewhere that a Scottish chieftain in
like circumstances divides the articles or their proceeds between
his two good followers, in proportion to the value from which
each has been separated. But I probably read it not in a law
book but in a romance.

X. It sounds more like Scott than Mansfield. But the idea
has its attractions. It is not so dour. It would save a lot of time
and litigation expense. To save is Scottish. However, as we do
not live in the mild Scottish legal climate, we must abandon
the fifty-fifty idea, and attempt to solve, as best we can, which
good man is to get one hundred and which good man is to get
zero.

W. Thank you for that. I now see clearly that, whether C or
D wins, the result is not against good conscience, — is not an
inequitable result. But I still do not see just what you meant
when you said that some of the transferability results disturbed
Williston as being opposed to the best interests of the business
community. Will you give me a specific example?

X. Yes. Suppose A owes B. For value received, B makes a
partial assignment of the debt to C.

W. And Williston thinks that C acquires only an equitable
interest in the debt?

X. That is his conception, and I agree with him.

W. I have not thought that out.

X. Later, B, the rascal, for value received, makes a total assignment of the debt to D, who has no notice of C's rights.

W. Similar problems would arise with sums due on a con-
tingency, as with insurance policies, I suppose?

X. Yes. It is a question of large practical importance. Williston conjectures that there are fully as many partial assignments
as total assignments. He thinks the needs of the business community require that the partial assignee be protected. I agree
with him.

W. Amen.

X. Now, if he adheres to the traditional common-law view,

the partial assignee is protected, for D will take only an equity in the debt and will be subject to the prior equity in C. And so Williston protects C, not because it would be against conscience to protect D, but because the needs of the business community require that C be protected.

This doctrine that the assignment is good 'in equity only' seems to me to be objectionable because it leaves the law in doubt in, say, ten per cent of the cases. If the restaters had been able to agree that as a general rule there should be legal assignability, but that this general rule should be subject to certain clearly defined exceptions, I should have gone along. But no such restatement has been made, and very likely it could not have been made without an abandonment, by some members of the composite unit, of principles which they felt that, in intellectual conscience, they could not abandon. But, the law not having been so clarified, I feel that the needs of the business community for reasonable certainty in the law require that in *all* cases there shall be legal assignability. At present, the law is in a shocking state of confusion.

W. Amen. As to the crying need of greater certainty in the law, and as to the mischievous consequences of leaving the law uncertain in, say, ten per cent of the cases, we see eye to eye. And I think that you would agree that not only is there need of greater certainty, but also of greater uniformity, and that this question of the assignability of rights to receive sums of money, when those rights are not evidenced by negotiable instruments, frequently arises in matters where many legal units are doing business in two or more states.

X. I agree heartily. On these matters there is not a bit of a shade of a shadow of a vestige of a trace of a scintilla of a possibility of a microscopic doubt of a complete agreement between us. These are questions of very great practical importance. That is why I am willing to go to the very verge of what seems to me to be permissible legal reasoning to attain the needed certainty and uniformity.

W. You think that I do more than to go to the verge, — that I go over the edge of the precipice?

X. Yes. I avert my eyes from what is to become of you. But I wish you a pleasant fall.

W. Let me tell you a gruesome tale. Once upon a time there was a prisoner in a grim, old fortress, built in Roman days, of contract conceptions. One black night he sought to escape by

the rope of legal power. Down he came, hand under hand, to
the end of his rope. His feet were swinging wildly. There were
jagged rocks below. He clung and clung, but came the moment
when he let go. You shudder?

X. I shudder.

W. He fell — one inch.

X. And therefore?

W. *Let go* the rope of legal power. You will come quickly,
pleasantly, painlessly to earth. Your feet will be on the solid
ground of legal title. At long last, your mind will be at peace, —
the perfect peace of a clear understanding. No longer will your
mental energies be drained by cautious, nice balancings.

X. You administer anaesthetics to your subject so that he
shall not realize that you are intruding into his vitals.

W. I thank you.

X. Almost thou persuadest me to be a legal titleist. But no.
I cannot, I must not. Get thee behind me. You are tempting
me to fall. It is the old, old, centuries-old plea that it will only
be such a *little* fall. No. God helping me, I shall not fall.

W. Then I must leave you in the air with below your feet a
yawning one-inch chasm.

A LECTURE IN CAMBRIDGE, ENGLAND

ON MAY 12, 1924, I gave a lecture, in the Hall of Corpus Christi,
to students in Cambridge University, England. The subject
matter of much of that lecture was published in 2 *Cambridge Law
Journal*, pages 180–191.

Thirty men decide to engage in the business of manufacturing
and selling bicycles. They procure the formation, under the
Companies (Consolidation) Act, 1908, of the X Bicycle Company, Limited. In the memorandum of association the objects
of the company are stated to be: 'The manufacture and sale of
bicycles.' The associates supply that legal unit with funds
through payment of subscriptions to its stock, and the company
proceeds to manufacture and sell bicycles. But the company
loses money, and, on the recommendation of the directors and
with the approval of all the shareholders, the manufacture of
bicycles is stopped, and the funds of the company are employed
in maintaining a motor omnibus service between two towns.

The driver of one of these omnibuses, while acting within the scope of his employment as prescribed by the directors of the company, by his negligence runs into A, who was at the time in the exercise of due care, and breaks A's leg. The driver is financially irresponsible. A sues the X Bicycle Company, Limited, and that company defends on the ground that maintaining the omnibus service was *ultra vires*. Should this defense be successful?

If one goes back far enough into English legal history, one will find that some bodies of men were recognized by the courts as legal units on the courts' own initiative. Men are constantly associating themselves together for some object or objects, as into firms or clubs or churches, and, in popular conception, these firms or clubs or churches are units, — composite units, to be sure, but nevertheless units. Now, in the nature of things, there is nothing to prevent the courts from recognizing, on their own initiative, such composite units as legal units, and it is interesting to find that at a very early date the courts did, on their own initiative, recognize some such bodies of men as legal units. But the rule gradually became established, and has now been recognized for centuries, that a body of men shall be recognized by the courts as a legal unit only if the Crown or Parliament has so ordered. For centuries the usual way in which a corporation was created was by a charter from the Crown, and Parliament rarely created a corporation prior to the nineteenth century. But for some time past the usual way in which corporations have been created has been by Act of Parliament, — either by a special Act incorporating a particular corporation or by a general Act which throws open the doors of incorporation to all who comply with the terms of the Act. A corporation created by charter is spoken of in the reports as a corporation at the common law. Chartered corporations, or corporations at the common law, are contrasted with statutory corporations.

Now, when the Crown chartered bodies of men, it chartered them for certain purposes only, — as to trade in a defined territory, or to search for certain metals, or to manufacture certain goods, or to supply a certain city with water, and so on. It is conceivable that the Crown should have given to a body of men the privilege of acting as a legal unit in any and all enterprises in which human beings might lawfully engage; but, query, if any such charter were ever granted. Similarly, when Parliament created corporations, either it itself stated the objects of the corporation created by special Act, or it required the incorporators to state the objects of the corporation which they were forming. That was so under the Companies Act, 1862, and it is so under the Companies (Consolidation) Act, 1908.

It will not be a misleading generalization to say that, with respect both to chartered corporations and to statutory corporations, the contemplated scope of corporate activity is defined. If we think of all occupations in which any human being may lawfully engage as a wide plain, it may be a helpful figure of speech to say that no corporation is given permission to wander over the whole plain, but each corporation is assigned to a bounded portion. Any act beyond the bounds is *ultra vires* of the corporation.

Can, then, a corporation do an *ultra vires* act?

The law is, and always has been, that a chartered corporation can do an *ultra vires* act. Indeed, if the Crown chartered a body of men, and, in the charter, the corporation was expressly commanded not to engage in a certain line of business, nevertheless the corporation did have legal capacity to engage in the prohibited business. Engaging in the prohibited business was beyond its legal authority; but not beyond its legal capacity. Engaging in such a prohibited business would, of course, be a wrong to the Crown, and would make the charter subject to forfeiture.

> The leading authority on this subject [said Mr. Justice Blackburn [1]] is the case of Sutton's Hospital.[2] There were many points raised in that case. Those which I think material to the present point arose on a part of the charter set out in the special verdict, by which the King incorporated the first governors of the Charterhouse, and expressly provided: 1. That they should have power to purchase, &c., as well goods, chattels, &c., as lands. 2. To sue, and be sued. 3. To have a common seal 'whereby the same corporation shall or may seal any manner of instrument touching the said corporation and the manor, lands, &c., thereto belonging, or in anywise touching or concerning the same. Nevertheless, it is our true intent and meaning that the said governors for the time being and their successors, nor any of them, shall do, or suffer to be done, at any time hereafter, any act or thing whereby or by means whereof any of the manors, &c., of the said incorporation or any estate, &c., shall be conveyed, &c., to any other whatsoever contrary to the true meaning hereof, other than by such leases as are hereafter mentioned, and that in such manner and form as is here-

[1] *Riche* v. *Ashbury Railway Carriage Co.*, L. R. Ex. 224, 262.   [2] 10 Co. 1.

after expressed and not otherwise.' The King, therefore, by this
charter not only did not in express terms give a power of alienation, but by express negative words forbad any alienation except
by lease. But the resolution of the Court, as reported by Coke (at
page 30b), was that 'when a corporation is duly created all other
incidents are *tacite* annexed;... and, therefore, divers clauses subsequent in the charter are not of necessity, but only declaratory,
and might well have been left out. As: 1. By the same to have
authority, ability and capacity to purchase; but no clause is
added that they may alien, &c., and it need not, for it is incident.
2. To sue and be sued, implead and be impleaded. 3. To have a
seal, &c.; that is also declaratory, for when they are incorporated
they may make or use what seal they will. 4. To restrain them
from aliening or demising, but in a certain form; that is an ordinance testifying the King's desire; but it is but a precept and doth
not bind in law.' This seems to me an express authority that at
common law it is an incident to a corporation to use its common
seal for the purpose of binding itself to anything to which a natural
person could bind himself, and to deal with its property as a
natural person might deal with his own. And further, that an
attempt to forbid this on the part of the King, even by express
negative words, does not bind at law. Nor am I aware of any authority in conflict with this case. If there are conditions contained
in the charter that the corporation shall not do particular things,
and these things are nevertheless done, it gives ground for a proceeding by *sci. fa.*, in the name of the Crown, to repeal the letters
patent creating the corporation: see *Reg.* v. *Eastern Archipelago
Company.*[3] But if the Crown take no such steps, it does not, as I
conceive, lie in the mouth either of the corporation, or of the person who has contracted with it, to say that the contract into which
they have entered was void as beyond the capacity of the corporation.

Other opinions to the same effect are mentioned in the margin.[4]

Is the law nevertheless that a statutory corporation has no legal
capacity to do an *ultra vires* act? Let me say at once that I
should not only concede, but urge, that a corporation might be
created by Parliament with no legal capacity to do an *ultra vires*
act. Parliament creates the corporation, it may mould its
creature as it pleases, and if it desires to create a corporation
with legal capacity to do only certain acts, of course it may do
so. And, if it sees fit to create a corporation with legal capacity

---

[3] 2 E. & B. 857.

[4] Archibald, J., reported in L. R. 9 Ex. 292; Bowen, L. J., reported 36 Ch. D. 685 n.;
Swinfen Eady, J., reported [1910] 1 Ch. 374.

to do only certain acts, then it of course follows that, even if all its members act in its name and with its funds in the doing of certain other acts, the courts must not give any corporate significance to those acts. A corporation acts through human beings, and the question whether a corporation has acted is always to be answered by inquiring (*a*) whether human beings have acted, and (*b*) whether it is proper to give corporate significance to their acts. The fundamental question in all corporation law is: To what acts of human beings shall corporate significance be given? In the case put, it would not be proper to give corporate significance to the acts of the members. *They*, the members, have acted; but *it*, the corporation, has not acted.

But let me also say that I should urge that it was equally clear that a corporation might be created by Parliament with legal capacity to do an *ultra vires* act. If the Crown can create corporations with legal capacity to do *ultra vires* acts, it would be extraordinary if Parliament could not. The only question for the courts is: What was the intent of Parliament? Did it intend to fashion any particular corporation on the model of the chartered corporation, in which case the corporation would have general legal capacity, or did it intend to create a legal unit with only special legal capacity? This is a question of statutory construction; it is not a question in the common law.

It may well be that the courts, in seeking to ascertain the intent of Parliament, may find some clear evidence that Parliament had before its mind the distinction between a corporation with general legal capacity and a corporation with special legal capacity, and that it chose to give the corporation in question only special legal capacity. But, if there is no such clear evidence, then I submit that the following three considerations are pertinent upon this question of statutory construction:

1. Chartered corporations are corporations at the common law. They have general legal capacity. The Legislature should be presumed to follow the common-law model rather than to depart from it.

2. The command of Parliament to a corporation not to act, except in pursuit of certain objects, should not be confused with, and be thought the same thing as, an expression of the intent of Parliament that that corporation shall not have legal capacity to act, except in pursuit of certain objects. The intent that there should be a lack of authority is very different from the intent that there should be a lack of capacity.

It is always to be remembered that legal capacity may be a capacity to incur obligations as well as a capacity to acquire rights, and the fact that Parliament has commanded a corporation to act only within a defined area does not at all prove that Parliament intended that, when the human beings who compose the corporation act in its name and with its funds outside the defined area, no corporate significance should be given to their acts.

To divert for a moment. Suppose it to be urged that a statutory corporation cannot commit a tort on this reasoning: Parliament in creating the corporation did not intend that it should commit a tort; the corporation can do only what Parliament has intended that it should do; therefore, the corporation cannot commit a tort. The answer to this reasoning is that, although the Legislature did not intend that the corporation should have authority to commit a tort, it did intend that it should have capacity to commit a tort. A command to the corporation to use only lawful means in attaining its objects is not equivalent to imposing a legal incapacity to use unlawful means. And, returning to our main question, when Parliament commands a corporation to act only in the pursuit of defined objects, it may well be that Parliament did not intend to impose a legal incapacity to act in the pursuit of other objects.

3. The practical consequences of holding that a corporation has no legal capacity to do an *ultra vires* act. Take the case put in the opening paragraph of this paper. The defense may be sustained on the ground that no corporate significance can be given to the act of the members of X in causing the motor omnibus to be run, because that would be contrary to Parliament's intent, but such a result would, I think, seem to most intelligent laymen to be plainly unjust. To expect that the law will always be comprehensible to intelligent laymen is perhaps too much; but, where there is room for two interpretations, the courts may properly assume that the Legislature did not intend a result which would seem to most intelligent laymen to be plainly unjust.

Having in mind all these considerations, it is submitted that the courts, when dealing with a statute of incorporation, ought to interpret that statute as conferring general legal capacity upon the corporation or corporations created thereby or thereunder, unless the intent of the Legislature is clear to confer special legal capacity only.

Let us now examine the opinion of Lord Cairns in *Ashbury Railway Carriage & Iron Co.* v. *Riche,*[5] respecting a company formed under the Companies Act, 1862. He said that there were four clauses in that statute to consider:

1. The sixth clause, which provided that 'Any seven or more persons associated for any lawful purpose may, by subscribing their names to a memorandum of association, and otherwise complying with the requisitions of this Act in respect of registration, form an incorporated company, with or without limited liability.' Lord Cairns remarked that this clause 'does not speak of that incorporation as the creation of a corporation with inherent common-law rights, such rights as are by common law possessed by every corporation, and without any other limit than would by common law be assigned to them, but it speaks of the company being incorporated with reference to a memorandum of association.'

2. The eighth clause, which provided that the memorandum of association should state, among other things, 'The objects for which the proposed company is to be established.' 'This being so,' said Lord Cairns, 'the existence, the coming into existence, of the company is to be an existence and to be a coming into existence for those objects and for those objects alone.'

3. The eleventh clause, which provided that the memorandum of association shall, when registered, 'bind the company and the members thereof to the same extent as if each member had subscribed his name and affixed his seal thereto, and there were in the memorandum contained, on the part of himself, his heirs, executors, and administrators, a covenant to observe all the conditions of such memorandum, subject to the provisions of this Act.' Lord Cairns remarked: 'That it is to be a covenant in which every member of the company is to covenant that he will observe the conditions of the memorandum, one of which is that the objects for which the company is established are the objects mentioned in the memorandum, and that he not only will observe that, but will observe it subject to the provisions of this Act.'

4. The twelfth clause, which provided that 'Any company limited by shares may so far modify the conditions contained in its memorandum of association, if authorized to do so by its regulations as originally framed, or as altered by special resolution in manner hereinafter mentioned, as to increase its capital

[5] L. R. 7 H. L. 653, 663.

by the issue of new shares of such amount as it thinks expedient, or to consolidate and divide its capital into shares of larger amount than its existing shares, or to convert its paid-up shares into stock; but, save as aforesaid, and save as is hereinafter provided in the case of a change of name, no alteration shall be made by any company in the conditions contained in the memorandum of association.' Lord Cairns remarked: 'The covenant, therefore, is not merely that every member will observe the conditions upon which the company is established, but that no change shall be made in those conditions; and if there is a covenant that no change shall be made in the objects for which the company is established, I apprehend that that includes within it the engagement that no object shall be pursued by the company, or attempted to be attained by the company in practice, except an object which is mentioned in the memorandum of association.'

From these four clauses in the statute, Lord Cairns's conclusions were:

It is a mode of incorporation which contains in it both that which is affirmative and that which is negative. It states affirmatively the ambit and extent of vitality and power which by law are given to the corporation, and it states, if it is necessary so to state, negatively, that nothing shall be done beyond that ambit, and that no attempt shall be made to use the corporate life for any other purpose than that which is so specified.... The memorandum of association is, as it were, the area beyond which the action of the company cannot go.... The question is as to the competency and power of the company to make the contract. Now, I am clearly of opinion that this contract was entirely, as I have said, beyond the objects in the memorandum of association. If so, it was thereby placed beyond the powers of the company to make the contract. ... If every shareholder of the company had been in the room, and every shareholder of the company had said, 'That is a contract which we desire to make, which we authorize the directors to make, to which we sanction the placing of the seal of the company,' the case would not have stood in any different position from that in which it stands now. The shareholders would thereby, by unanimous consent, have been attempting to do the very thing which, by the Act of Parliament, they were prohibited from doing.... It was the intention of the Legislature, not implied, but actually expressed, that the corporation should not enter, having regard to its memorandum of association, into a contract of this description.

All would agree that it was the intention of the Legislature that the corporation 'should' not act, except to attain the objects stated in its memorandum of association. Plainly, there was a lack of legal authority to do any other acts. But was there a lack of legal capacity? The remarks of Lord Cairns have been quoted at considerable length to show that he did not have the distinction between legal authority and legal capacity clearly in mind. He made 'It can not' to follow upon 'It should not.'

The four clauses of the Companies Act upon which Lord Cairns relied required the registered memorandum of association (which, as he himself says,[6] 'is, as it were, the charter') to state 'the objects' of the company, made no provision for an amendment respecting the objects, and required the members to covenant to observe all the conditions of such memorandum. Such provisions, it is submitted, furnish an insufficient basis for concluding that the Legislature intended that, even if all the members of the company acted in its name and with its funds to do an act outside the defined objects, no corporate significance should attach. A memorandum of association was required, but some principal organization paper — some substitute for a charter — would naturally be required, irrespective of whether the Legislature intended to limit authority or capacity. The memorandum of association must state 'the objects,' but this was in accordance with, not in contrast to, the practice of the Crown in granting charters. There was no provision for a change in the objects; but neither had it been customary for the Crown to provide for any change in the objects specified in charters (and, moreover, a natural explanation of this provision is that the Legislature intended to protect minorities from changes desired by majorities). The members covenant to observe all the conditions of the memorandum; but it is difficult to see anything in this to show that the Legislature intended to limit legal capacity. Indeed, the argument would rather be the other way, for if the company *could* not act except to attain the defined objects, by reason of the fact that the Legislature itself had so limited its capacity, why require covenants from the members that the company shall not so act?

The question whether a particular corporation has general legal capacity or only special legal capacity must be answered by correctly interpreting the statute whereby or whereunder it was created. For reasons set forth above, it is submitted that

[6] L. R. 7 H. L. 668.

the courts, when dealing with a statute of incorporation, ought to interpret that statute as conferring general legal capacity upon the corporation or corporations created thereby or thereunder, unless the intent of the Legislature is clear to confer special legal capacity only. If that mode of approach is adopted, it is now further submitted that the Companies Act, 1862, contains no clear evidence of an intent by Parliament to confer special legal capacity only upon the corporations created thereunder.

It remains to inquire, the decision of the House of Lords in *Ashbury Railway Carriage & Iron Company* v. *Riche* having been what it was, whether a court which is bound by that decision may properly give the plaintiff relief in the case stated in the opening paragraph of this paper.

In the *Ashbury Company* case the plaintiff sought damages for the breach of an *ultra vires* contract; in the case stated in the opening paragraph of this paper the plaintiff is seeking damages for a tort committed in the course of an *ultra vires* undertaking. As an original question, it would have been easy to distinguish the two cases. The statute might have been construed as conferring general legal capacity upon a corporation created thereunder. Then the corporation would have capacity both to make an *ultra vires* contract and to commit a tort in the course of an *ultra vires* undertaking. But clearly it would have no authority to do either. In the *Ashbury Company* case the plaintiff knew, or ought to have known, that the company was making a contract which it had no authority to make; that this was, as against the State, an offense; and that the performance of the contract would involve a diversion of corporate assets which might be harmful to non-assenting present shareholders, to future shareholders who bought shares without a knowledge of the facts, and to creditors who had extended, or should thereafter extend, credit to the company, believing that its funds would be employed only in the pursuit of the objects stated in the memorandum of association. On these grounds the plaintiff should fail, — not because the company could not make the contract, but because the company ought not to have made the contract, and the plaintiff knew, or ought to have known, that fact; so that he has voluntarily participated in improper corporate action. In the tort case, on the other hand, the plaintiff has himself done nothing wrong; he is the victim of a wrongful act, and the only question is whether corporate significance may properly be attached to that act.

The result of the *Ashbury Company* case may be accepted, and nevertheless relief be given to the plaintiff in the tort case. But I am unable to see how the reasoning of the court (the opinion of Lord Cairns ought to be recognized as the leading opinion, with the reasoning of which on this point the other Lords were content) may be accepted, and nevertheless relief be given to the plaintiff in the tort case. The thought of Lord Cairns was that the area of corporate activity was defined by the statement of the objects, and that there could be no corporate activity except in that area. That is equivalent to saying that the company has no capacity to do an *ultra vires* act. It no more has capacity to commit a tort in the course of an *ultra vires* undertaking than to make a contract in the course of that undertaking.

It is true that the Companies (Consolidation) Act, 1908, differs somewhat from the Companies Act, 1862, since there is a provision permitting, within limits, alteration of the memorandum of association with respect to the objects of the company,[7] and, since considerable stress was laid by Lord Cairns on the fact that, in the Companies Act, 1862, there could be no alteration in the objects, there is a basis for contending that a company formed under the 1908 Act has a wider legal capacity than a company formed under the 1862 Act. But in *Baroness Wenlock* v. *River Dee Company*,[8] counsel sought to distinguish the incorporating statute there in question from the Companies Act, and Lord Blackburn said: 'The course the argument took makes me think it is proper to say — though it is quite true, as Mr. Rigby said, that it was not necessary for the decision in *Ashbury Company* v. *Riche* to do more than decide what the law was with regard to a company formed under the Companies Act of 1862 — that I think the law there laid down applies to all companies created by any statute for a particular purpose. I think that if I were to confine the effect of the decision to companies created under the Act of 1862 and to say it did not extend to such a corporation as this, I should do wrong. The law is proverbially uncertain. That cannot be helped. But I think I should unjustifiably add to the uncertainty if I set an example of adhering to my previous reasoning [9] (even should I still think it better than that of noble and learned Lords who decided against it), in every case not precisely involving the very same point.'

[7] Section 9.   [8] L. R. 10 A. C. 354, 360.
[9] In *Riche* v. *Ashbury Co.*, L. R. 9 Ex. 254.

If the law be that no company created by any statute for a particular purpose has capacity to do any act except in pursuit of its stated objects, then judgment must be given for the defendant in the case put in the opening paragraph of this paper.

It is proper, however, to say that there would seem to be no decision as to torts which requires this result,[10] and to call at-

[10] In *Poulton* v. *The London and South Western Ry. Co.*, L. R. 2 Q. B. 534, the defendant was held not liable for the act of one of its stationmasters for causing the arrest of a passenger who he erroneously believed had, without justification, failed to pay for the carriage of a horse. By Act of Parliament, the defendant was empowered to give into custody a passenger who did not pay his fare, but was not empowered to give into custody a passenger who did not pay for the carriage of goods. The court held that the act of the stationmaster was not within the scope of his authority. Blackburn, J., said: 'In the present case an act was done by the stationmaster completely out of the scope of his authority, which there can be no possible ground for supposing the railway company authorized him to do, and a thing which could never be right on the part of the company to do. Having no power themselves, they cannot give the stationmaster any power, to do the act.' Mellor, J., said: 'It limits the scope of authority, to be implied from the fact of being the stationmaster, to such acts as the company could do themselves, and I cannot think it ever can be implied that the company authorized the stationmaster to do that which they have no authority to do themselves.' Shee, J., said: 'An authority cannot be implied to have been given to a servant to do an act, which, if his master were on the spot, the master would not be justified in doing.' Right, power, authority are used by the judges as though they were interchangeable terms. The case decides that the implied authority of a stationmaster does not extend to the doing of acts which are *ultra vires* of the company, and it would seem that Sir John Salmond is right in his contention that it decided no more than that. (Salmond, on the Law of Torts, 3rd, p. 59.) The court was not called upon to decide, and did not decide, that the corporation had no legal capacity to commit an *ultra vires tort*.

In *Mill* v. *Hawker*, L. R. 9 Ex. 309, the plaintiff sued the members of an incorporated highway board (25 & 26 Vict., c. 61) for a trespass done to his property by a surveyor who acted pursuant to an order which the members purported to have made in their corporate capacity, and the court held the defendants liable (Kelly, C.B., dissenting). Cleasby, B., with whom Pigott, B., concurred, said: 'But it is equally clear that when the acts are such as the corporate body is not by law qualified to do, and the corporate body, if they pretend to do them, are acting *ultra vires*, then the mere fact of giving a corporate form to the act does not prevent it from being the act of those who cause it to be done. It seems plain that in such a case the individuals and not the corporation really do the act, and no authority is needed for that conclusion.' The learned Baron proceeded to point out that the effect of holding that such a body as the highway board were competent in their corporate capacity to commit such an act would be to cause the damages to be paid out of funds which ought to be applied in maintaining the roads, that the persons eventually responsible would be the ratepayers, and among them, perhaps, the persons entitled to redress, and to whom the damages were to be paid, and that thus the members of the highway board would acquire a power to divert and waste the funds entrusted to them for public purposes. Moreover, that it would appear to be only right, if the burden of such damages and costs were to fall upon the ratepayers at all, that they should be paid by the parish in which the road in question was situated, and that, owing to the constitution of the board, the persons who ordered the trespass might be persons representing other parishes in the district, and not the parish wherein the road was situated.

Kelly, C.B., said: 'I conceive it to be settled law that no action lies against the intention (*a*) to one decision, and (*b*) to one statement by a learned author which might at least arouse hope in counsel for the plaintiff.

(*a*) *In re David Payne and Company, Limited.*[11] The directors of David Payne and Company, Limited, borrowed money by issuing a debenture in the name of the company. They intended to apply, and did apply, this money in the name of the company to accomplish an object outside the objects of the company, as stated in its memorandum of association; but the lender did not know, and could not have been expected to know, of the intended misapplication. The court said: 'A corporation cannot do anything except for the purposes of its business, borrowing or anything else; everything else is beyond its power, and is *ultra vires.*' Nevertheless, the court held that the debenture was a valid obligation against the company. If a company cannot borrow except for the purposes of its business, it is difficult to see how debentures evidencing loans procured, not for the purposes of its business, are obligations against the company. Borrowing, not for the purposes of the company, is an act in 'the area beyond which the action of the company cannot go.' The court announced that the company could not do this sort of thing, but then, considering the hardship to the plaintiff of a decision against him, concluded that the company had done it. The court paid lip service to the special capacity reasoning, but did not logically apply that reasoning. It reached the result which would have been reached by holding that the company had general capacity to borrow, but a limited authority, and finding that the plaintiff had no notice of the lack of authority in the particular case.

dividual members of a corporation for a corporate act done by the corporation in its corporate capacity, unless the act be maliciously done by the individuals charged, and the corporate name be used as a mere color for the malicious act, or unless the act is *ultra vires,* and is not, and cannot be in contemplation of law, a corporate act at all,' but he thought the order of the board in question could not properly be said to be *ultra vires,* as it was an act 'merely unlawful or unauthorized.'

From this decision, it would appear that all the judges conceived that there might be a wrongful act done in the name of the corporation at the instigation of its members to which no corporate significance could be attached. But, assuming that the majority was right in considering that the act in question was such an act, the decision would not be very persuasive as to a corporation organized under the Companies Act. For the protection of the ratepayers, the Legislature may well have intended that the legal capacity of such a corporation as this highway board, formed for public purposes and empowered to expend money raised by taxation, should be strictly limited, and it would be entirely consistent that it should have a different intent with respect to a private business corporation, organized for the financial benefit of its members.

[11] [1904] 2 Ch. 608.

(b) Sir John Salmond, in the second edition of his work on the *Law of Torts*, published in 1910, said:[12] 'A corporation, however, is not liable for the torts of its servants or agents (even in cases in which individual persons would be liable) unless the authority committed to those servants or agents is *intra vires* of the corporation. . . . A corporation *cannot* authorize anything to be done, except within the limits allowed by law to the corporate action of that particular body. Any authority given beyond these limits is *ultra vires* and void; the acts done under it are not attributed by the law to the corporation, and therefore the corporation cannot be held liable for them.' But in his third edition, published in 1912, he said:[13] 'The rule that a corporation is not bound by contracts which are *ultra vires* is commonly said to apply also to torts which are *ultra vires*, in the sense that they are committed in the course of some activity which is beyond the limits of the corporation's powers. There is, however, no sufficient authority for any such exemption of corporations from the consequences of their disregard of the limits of their powers. It seems contrary to principle, and has been decisively rejected in numerous American decisions. . . . The true principle is, it is submitted, the following: Every act done, authorized, or ratified on behalf of a corporation by the supreme governing authority of that corporation, or by any person or body of persons to whom the general powers of the corporation are delegated, is, for the purpose of the law of torts, the act of the corporation itself, whether *intra vires* or *ultra vires* of the corporation, and the corporation is liable accordingly for that act or for any tort committed in respect of it by any agent or servant of the corporation within the scope of his authority or employment.' These statements reappear in the later editions.

To say that a corporation *has* disregarded the limits of its powers is to beg the fundamental question whether it has legal capacity to act except in a defined area. And whether a statutory corporation has such capacity is not a question of 'principle,' in the sense of being a question at the common law, — it is a question of the correct interpretation of the particular incorporating statute.

It may be interesting to note that in most decisions in America, the courts have reached conclusions which logically involved

[12] Chap. II, Sec. 18, p. 56.
[13] Chap. II, Sec. 18, pp. 58, 59, 60.

holding that the corporation in question did have legal capacity to do an *ultra vires* act, if the act in question was a tort to the plaintiff.[14]

SERJEANTS–AT–LAW; THE ORDER OF THE COIF

Written for the *Virginia Law Review*, May, 1942

IN THE DAYS of Victoria a serjeant-at-law, one of the foremost English barristers and a friend of the Prince of Wales, was asked by the colonel of a crack regiment to dine one night with him and the other officers. At the appointed time he presented himself at the appointed place. 'What name, sir?' asked the orderly. 'Serjeant Asterisk.' The orderly drew himself up and back, aghast. 'This is an *officers*' mess. Where the non-commissioned officers eat, I have no idea.'

There are few persons alive today who have an adequate conception of the unbridgeable gulf that divided a serjeant-at-law from a sergeant. Sergeants were persons such as a sergeant in the army ('This is the sergeant Who like a good and hardy soldier fought.' *Macbeth*, I, ii, 3, 4); a sergeant in a police force ('The force consisted of three inspectors, nine sergeants, and a body of police termed "plain-clothes men."' Wynter, *Curiosities of Civilization*, p. 469); a member of the bodyguard of a court or magistrate (in the thirty-fifth verse of the sixteenth chapter of the Acts of the Apostles it was written: 'And when it was day, the magistrates sent the serjeants, saying, Let those men go'); or an officer of a court, like the present-day American deputy sheriff, charged with the duty of making arrests or levying executions upon property ('This fell sergeant, Death, Is strict in his arrest.' *Hamlet*, V, ii, 347, 348).

The preferable spelling is ser*j*eant for serjeants-at-law (Coke steadily used that spelling), and ser*g*eant for those charged with such functions as those indicated above. But even this difference in spelling has not always been observed. It is surprising to find that Johnson in his Dictionary gave no word 'serjeant,' and put a sergeant-at-law as one species of the genus 'sergeant'; and the Bible, as shown above, speaks of members of the bodyguard of magistrates as serjeants. This difference in spelling

[14] See cases collected in Warren, *Cases on Corporations*, 2nd ed., pp. 677–685.

has, however, usually been observed for at least a century by careful writers.

Serjeants-at-law were awe-inspiring personages. They fed the Bench; they led the Bar; they were in an inner circle of the Great Men of the Realm.

A serjeant was the servant of the Sovereign. Serjeant-at-law was the English equivalent of the Latin *serviens ad legem*. We shall begin to appreciate the great dignity and importance of the title if we compare those persons who were serjeants-at-law with those persons who in the feudal days held land in fee simple from the Sovereign by the tenure of serjeanty. That was the most honorable of all tenures.

Littleton said: 'Tenure by grand serjeanty is, where a man holds his lands or tenements of our sovereign lord the king by such services as he ought to do in his proper person to the king, as to carry the banner of the king, or his lance, or to lead his army, or to be his marshall, or to carry his sword before him at his coronation, or to be his sewer [i.e., server and, perhaps, taster] at his coronation, or his carver, or his butler, or to be one of his chamberlaines of the receipt of his exchequer, or to do other like services, &c.'[1] 'Tenure by petite serjeanty is, where a man holds his land of our soveraigne lord the king, to yield to him yearly a bow or a sword, or a dagger, or a knife, or a lance, or a paire of gloves of maile, or a paire of gilt spurs, or an arrow, or divers arrowes, or to yield such other small things belonging to warre.'[2] And Coke, commenting upon these sections, said: '*Serjeantia idem est quod servitium.* And it is called *magna serjeantia*, or *serjanteria*, or *magnum servitium*, great service, as well in respect of the excellency and greatnesse of the person to whom it is to be done (for it is to be done to the king only) as of the honour of the service itselfe,' and Coke proceeds to show how petite serjeanty differs from grand serjeanty only in that in grand serjeanty the service must be done by the tenant *in person*, while the bow, or sword, or dagger was not necessarily delivered by the tenant in person.[3]

Serjeants-at-law were likewise servants of the Sovereign. It was their duty to assist the Sovereign in the administration of his law. War was first, but law was an honored second.

Serjeants-at-law were usually, if not always, gentry. And many of their descendants were ennobled. The number of instances in which this occurred is large, surprisingly large. I will

[1] *Tenures*, sec. 153.   [2] *Id.*, sec. 159.   [3] Co. Litt. 105b, 108a.

mention only four. The Duke of Norfolk is a descendant of William Howard, created a serjeant-at-law in 1287; the Duke of Devonshire is a descendant of John de Cavendish, created a serjeant-at-law in 1366; descendants of Littleton (or Lyttleton), created a serjeant-at-law in 1453, became Lord Lyttleton of Frankley and Lord Lyttleton of Moonslow; and descendants of Coke, created a serjeant-at-law in 1606, became Earls of Leicester.

Serjeants-at-law were for many centuries outstanding figures in English law in no less than six ways:

1. They were the reservoir from which the judges of the highest courts were drawn. From a very early date down through the centuries to 1875, no one was made a Chief Justice or other Justice of the King's Bench, or a Chief Justice or other Justice of the Court of Common Pleas, or a Chief Baron of the Court of Exchequer, who was not a Brother of the Coif.[4] And some of the Barons of the Court of Exchequer and several of the Chancellors have also been of the Coif.

2. They, equally with the judges of the High Courts, were commissioned to 'ride the circuit.' For centuries commissions to serve as itinerant judges or judges of assize could by statute only be given either to judges *or* to serjeants-at-law.[5]

Some of the circuit commissions seem to have had no names in the quorum except practising serjeants-at-law, who were on such occasions the *only* judges of assize.[6]

3. Out of the general body of the serjeants-at-law a few were selected as King's (or Queen's) Serjeants. They were *Servientes Regis ad legem.*[7]

The list of King's Serjeants includes some famous names. For example, Littleton was made a King's Serjeant two years after he had been made a serjeant-at-law, and it may be noted that Cromwell made Maynard, that giant among barristers, 'Lord Protector's Serjeant.'[8]

They were counsel to the Sovereign and also acted as public prosecutors. The Solicitor-General and even the Attorney-General were *inferior* Crown officers. Coke's position as

---

[4] See Preface, xxiv, to 10 Co. Rep., 4th Inst. 75, 99; see also 2 Rot. Parl. 331b.

[5] See 14 Edw. III, c. 16. This policy was continued until 1850 — see 13 & 14 Vict. c. 25.

[6] Pulling, *Order of the Coif*, p. 38.

[7] The serjeant-at-law made a King's (or Queen's) Serjeant was declared by the Sovereign, even in the reign of Victoria, to be 'one of *our* Serjeants-at-Law.'

[8] See Wynne's *Miscellany*, pp. 256, 291.

Attorney-General to Queen Elizabeth and James I did *not* give him the first position at the English Bar.

At the assizes in every county the King's Serjeant had all the powers which the Attorney-General now has. Even in early Victorian days, the form of proclamation was: 'If any one can inform my Lords the Queen's Justices, the Queen's Attorney-General, or the Queen's Serjeant, of any treasons, murders, felonies or misdemeanours,' etc.

4. All serjeants-at-law owed a duty to serve as counsel to the King's *subjects*. Of this, much more hereafter.

5. They were in early times not infrequently summoned to aid Parliament on difficult questions of law.[9]

6. They were the recognized authorities on Parliamentary law. Several of them were made Speaker of the House of Commons.

The number of the Brothers of the Coif throughout the centuries was small, — very small. I doubt if the number of *practising* serjeants-at-law (that is, the total number of members of the Order of the Coif, less those who had been elevated to the bench) averaged through the centuries to be more than a dozen.[10]

By an ordinance of Edward I,[11] headed '*De Attornatis & Apprenticiis*,' the Sovereign directed the Justices of the Common Bench to select a certain number from every county '*de melioribus & legalioribus & libentius addiscentibus, secundum quod intellexerint qd̂ Curie sue & Popul' de Regno melius valere poterit, & majus commodum fuerit. Et quod ipsi quos ad hoc elegerint Cur' sequantur, et se de negotiis in eadem Cur' intromittant, et alii non.*' It seemed to the King and his Council that seven score should be sufficient, but the determination of the precise number was left to the discretion of the justices.

It is to be noted that the seven score were to include all attorneys and apprentices. Attorneys correspond to the modern solicitors, and apprentices to the modern barristers. 'Apprentices' was the name given for centuries to *all* barristers, other than those who were Brothers of the Coif. A lawyer might have practised for many years and be renowned for his profound learning in the law and for his consummate skill in advocacy, but nevertheless he was, until created a serjeant-at-law, only

[9] 1 Rot. Parl. 346a, 2 *id.* at 185b, 3 *id.* at 101b. A serjeant-at-law is said to have drawn the Statute *De Donis*.

[10] Many details are given in Wynne's *Miscellany*, pp. 244–354.

[11] 1 Rot. Parl. 84b.

an 'apprentice.' Plowden, although created a serjeant-at-law,[12] is described on the title-page of his *Commentaries* (first edition, 1571) as 'Edmunde Plowden un apprentice de le comen Ley,' — possibly that is evidence of a relish for understatement. Coke himself, throughout the time that he was Attorney-General to Queen Elizabeth and her cousin James I, was not a serjeant-at-law, but only an 'apprentice.' And Coke, speaking of the Barons of the Exchequer who were not Brothers of the Coif, said:[13]

> Of these Serjeants, as of the seminary of justice, are chosen Judges; for none can be a Judge, either of the Court of King's Bench, or of the Common Pleas, or Chief Baron of the Exchequer, unless he be a Serjeant; neither can he be of either of the Serjeants Inns, unless he hath been a Serjeant at Law; for it is not called Judges or Justices Inn, but Serjeants Inn; for I have known Barons of the Exchequer (that were not of the coif, and yet had judicial places and voices) remain in the houses of court whereof they were fellows, and *wore the habit of apprentices of law.*' (Italics supplied.)

With this limitation on the number of all solicitors *and* barristers, it naturally followed that the number of that innermost circle of the barristers, the Brothers of the Coif, should be very small.

At the beginning of Mr. Serjeant Pulling's excellent treatise on the Order of the Coif there is a table in which are listed alphabetically all the serjeants-at-law created from 1164 to 1875. The total number was only a little over a thousand, so that during those seven centuries the number created averaged only three in two years.

My secretary tells me that the number of serjeants-at-law created in each reign was as given below. Where there was a demise of the Crown in any year, all creations were ascribed to the incoming Sovereign.

Henry II (1154–1189), thirteen
Richard I (1189–1199), six
John (1199–1216), six
Henry III (1216–1272), thirty-six
Edward I (1272–1307), thirty-four
Edward II (1307–1326), eighteen
Edward III (1326–1377), fifty-seven
Richard II (1377–1399), twenty-one

---

[12] He was summoned by writ in 6 Philip and Mary. Mary died before the writ was returnable. But he was again summoned in 1 Elizabeth, and I see no reason to doubt that he then took the oath.

[13] Preface, xli, xlii, to 10 Co. Rep.

Henry IV (1399–1413), fifteen
Henry V (1413–1422), fifteen
Henry VI (1422–1461), thirty-two
Edward IV (1461–1483), twenty-six
Edward V (1483–1483), none
Richard III (1483–1485), none
Henry VII (1485–1509), thirty
Henry VIII (1509–1547), forty-five
Edward VI (1547–1553), fourteen
Philip and Mary (1553–1558), ten
Elizabeth (1558–1603), sixty-three
James I (1603–1625), fifty-one
Charles I (1625–1649), sixty-three
The Commonwealth (1649–1660), nine-
teen
Charles II, after the Restoration and
until his death (1660–1685), ninety-
five
James II (1685–1689), nineteen
William and Mary (1689–1702), forty-
three
Anne (1702–1714), twenty
George I (1714–1727), thirty-five
George II (1727–1760), fifty-two
George III (including the Regency,
1760–1820), eighty-eight
George IV (1820–1830), twenty-three
William IV (1830–1837), eleven
Victoria (from 1837 to 1875 when the
last appointments were made),
eighty-six

So much by way of introduction. The remainder of the article
is divided into the following seven parts:

I. The Antiquity of the Order of the Coif.
II. The Coif.
III. The Relation of the Order of the Coif to the Court of
Common Pleas.
IV. The Relation of the Order of the Coif to the Inns of
Court.
V. The Relation of the Order of the Coif to Saint Paul's
Cathedral.
VI. The Selection of Serjeants-at-law, and the Ceremonies
Incident to their Creation.
VII. The Decline and Fall of the Order of the Coif.

I. The Antiquity of the Order of the Coif.

It has been said that there was an Order of the Coif even before the Norman Conquest. Is such statement warranted?

The English serjeants-at-law, of which we can feel sure, were all created by writ of the Sovereign under the Great Seal, resembling the writ of summons used in the creation of peers. This writ is one of the very earliest writs of which we have any record. Coke gives the form of the writ,[14] and that form continued without substantial change into the nineteenth century. The form of the writ as used in the early Victorian days was as follows:

> Victoria, by the grace of God, of the United Kingdom of Great Britain and Ireland Queen,[15] Defender of the Faith, to our trusty and well-beloved A. B. of [say] the Inner Temple, London, Esq., greeting. Forasmuch as, by the advice of our Council, we have ordained you to take upon you the state and degree of a Serjeant-at-law without delay, we strictly enjoining command you to put in order and prepare yourself to take upon you the state and degree aforesaid, in form aforesaid, and this you may in nowise omit under the pain of one thousand pounds. Witness ourselves at Westminster the   day of   , in the year of our reign.

We shall see in a moment that Henry II (1154–1189) issued about a dozen such writs, but the issue of such writs was very rarely, if ever, made before his reign.

What evidence is there that there was an Order of the Coif before the issue of such writs and even before the Norman Conquest?

There is in the Harvard Law Library a rare and treasured manuscript (probably dating from about 1300) of the Grand Coutumier de Normandie. Pretty surely this stems from a collection of the ancient customs of Normandy made upon the direction of Henry II, and those customs were (at least usually) customs which had existed for centuries. In this manuscript we find the following:

> De pledeors. **LX.** Cels sunt apeles pledeors qui meinent q̄reles en cort en demandant et en defendāt.
>
> De conteors. **LXI.** Cels sunt apeles conteors que aucuns esta-

---

[14] Preface, xxxix, to 10 Co. Rep.

[15] Victoria assumed the additional title of Empress of India in 1876, but no serjeants-at-law were created after that date.

blissent a conter por els en cort. Si doiuent ses paroles autretât
valoir come sil iessoient de la bouche a cels q̄ les atornerent.

There is satisfactory evidence that serjeants-at-law were regarded as the successors of the Norman *conteurs*. Certain it is,
that they were repeatedly called *contors* or *serjeant-counters*.[16]
So the question narrows to this: Were the Norman conteurs a
brotherhood which had adopted the coif as their distinctive
emblem?

It may well be. It was usual in those days for persons engaged
in any particular kind of activity to join together, for the purposes of mutual protection and control, into brotherhoods or
guilds. It was also usual in those days for the brotherhoods
or guilds to adopt some emblem, very often an article of dress,
as distinctive of the members of the brotherhoods or guilds.
Possibly, the coif was first worn in the time of Henry II, but the
probability is the other way. Probably, it had for centuries
been worn by lawyers of the class of conteurs, so that the issue
of writs to serjeants-at-law did not have the creative consequence
of introducing the use of the coif, but, rather, had the restrictive
consequence of making (either immediately or after a lapse of
time) its use unlawful by anyone not summoned by the writ of
the Sovereign to be a serjeant-at-law. Possibly, Henry II commanded his serjeants-at-law to use the coif; but probably the
serjeants-at-law adopted on their own motion a distinctive
emblem, and they adopted the coif as such emblem because it
had been used by the conteurs, a class of lawyers not dissimilar
to themselves, time out of mind. I therefore conclude that
probably (although not surely) there was a Brotherhood of the
Coif in Normandy before 1066 and in England after that date
and before the time of Henry II.

But when we come to the reign of Henry II (1154–1189),
we pass out of the realm of conjecture. He summoned about a
dozen serjeants-at-law, and probably they adopted the coif as
their distinctive emblem. It continued to be the distinctive
emblem until the Order of the Coif (in England) became extinct.

---

[16] See Co. Litt. 17a; 2d Inst. 214; the Preface, ix, to 9 Co. Rep.; and the Preface,
xxxv, to 10 Co. Rep.

It should, however, be noted that there is a serious difference of opinion as to the
reliability of the Mirror of Justices mentioned in the Preface, iii, ix, to 9 Co. Rep. Although it professes to state the law from a time antedating the Norman Conquest, it
was probably not written until long after that Conquest.

See also Reeves's *History of English Law*, vol. II, p. 358.

The serjeants-at-law summoned by Henry II were as follows:

1168, Reginald de Warenne.
1174, John de Cumin, William Fitz Ralph, and William Fitz-
    Stephen.
1176, William Basset, and Roger Fitz Reinfrid.
1177, Hugh de Cressy.
1179, Hugh de Gaerst, Ranulph de Glanvil, and Hugh Murdac.
1182, William de Auberville and Osbert Fitz Hervey.
1184, Ralph Fitz-Stephen.

If the existence of anything could be traced back as far as 1189, such thing was said to be of immemorial antiquity.[17] I think that it is clear that the Order of the Coif in England existed before 1189, and that therefore it is of immemorial antiquity.

It was the earliest Order in England which owed its creation to the Sovereign. The Most Noble Order of the Garter was not instituted until at least 1330, — compared with the Coif, the Garter was *nouveau*.

II. *The Coif.*

A coif is a headdress (cf. a lady's coiffure). At first, the coif covered the whole head, except the face, and was kept in place by ligaments tied under the chin. It closely resembled, except for the material, a Knight's helmet (coif *de fer*), and the Heralds' College emphasized the similarity between helmet and coif.

It was white in color, and was probably of silk or lawn. Thus in the *Vision of Piers the Plowman* there are these lines:

> Conscience and the kyng in-to the court wenten,
> Where houede an hondred in houes of silke,
> Seriauntes hij semede that seruen atte barre,
> To plede for penyes and poundes the lawe.[18]

> Shal no seriaunte for that seruys were a selk houe,
> Ne pelour in hus paueylon for pledying at the barre.[19]

'Houve,' according to Murray's *New English Dictionary*, was 'a covering for the head; a turban, a coif'; etc.

---

[17] In 3 Edw. I, c. 39 (1275), it was provided 'that in conveying a descent in a writ of right, none shall presume to declare of the seisin of his ancestor further, or beyond the time of King Richard.' Richard I came to the throne in 1189, and the English courts in other matters adopted 1189 as the date when, as it is sometimes put, 'legal memory began.'

[18] Skeat ed., c. i, 158–161 (vol. I, p. 15).

[19] *Id.*, c. iv, 451, 452 (vol. I, p. 97).

Perhaps the earliest available representation of the coif is the picture of the pleader with the coif in the frontispiece of Sayles, *Select Cases in the Court of King's Bench* (Selden Society), vol. I.

In my treatise on *Margin Customers* (1941) there is, opposite page 44, a portrait of Littleton. He is wearing an old-fashioned coif, which to a modern eye looks more or less like a night-cap. It appears from numerous effigies and pictures that the serjeants-at-law continued to wear this kind of coif well into the sixteenth century.

There is an engraving of the Court of Wards and Liveries in the time of Elizabeth of which many copies seem to be in existence. In a copy which hangs upon a wall in Langdell Hall, we read that it probably represents that court in session about 1585; that the first figure at the left side (as one faces the picture) is of a Queen's Serjeant; and that the two figures at the bottom, standing outside the Bar, are of two serjeants-at-law. These two serjeants have a white covering over the top of the head and coming down to the ears (but not below). There are no ligaments under the chin. But the Queen's Serjeant has a head-covering of black, with only a narrow edging of white. There is a portrait of Sir Francis Moore (1558–1621), probably made about 1614, where he, a serjeant-at-law (but not a King's Serjeant), has the same kind of headdress as did the Queen's Serjeant in 1585. In *Margin Customers*, opposite page 52, is a portrait of Coke, which dates from about 1616. In the pictures of 1585 and 1614, the black cap was a close-fitting skull-cap, but Coke's cap has a body and wings, — more like a rather fancy modern golf cap than a skull-cap. Now Coke delighted in good clothes well worn, and it may be that he set a fashion, — there are later portraits of other serjeants-at-law where the black cap has a full body and is not a mere skull-cap. Coke's cap had trimmings of white at both sides (but not over the brow).

After the Restoration of Charles II, the French fashion of wearing wigs came in, and wigs were worn not simply by lawyers but by all men of fashion. The judges and barristers adopted the prevailing fashion; they were by no means the leaders in adopting the fashion; they are different from other men only in that they have continued to wear wigs long after other men had dropped the fashion with its Louis XIV connotations. But — probably in order not to break wholly from the traditions of the past — there was a little spot of white on the top (say, two or three inches in diameter) with an inner circle of black. This, so far as I know, was the last form of the headdress of a serjeant-at-law.

Note that the white was never wholly dispensed with. The touch of white is the *sine qua non* of the headdress of the later serjeants-at-law.

The black cap worn by Coke and many others (with its touch or touches of white) should not be confused with the black *sentence cap*. The black cap (with its touch or touches of white) was a day-to-day headdress. The black sentence cap was put on when a judge was about to pronounce sentence of death, and was rarely, if ever, *worn* at other times. But it was a recognized part of the habiliments of a judge and was carried in the hand on some ceremonial occasions.

The wearing of the coif was obligatory in court and on any ceremonial occasion. And it will aid to a just appraisal of the dignity of a serjeant-at-law if we note that the serjeant remained covered in the Presence of Majesty. 'Neither shall a *Judge*, or a Serjeant at Law, take off the said *Coif* tho' he be in the Royal Presence and talking with the King's Majesty.' [20]

III. The Relation of the Order of the Coif to the Court of Common Pleas.

William the Conqueror (and subsequent sovereigns) assembled from time to time the Great Men of the Realm. This assemblage was often called the *Curia Regis*. It was an amorphous, royally catholic body. The members might be called upon to advise and assist the Sovereign in *any* matter affecting the realm, — military, diplomatic, political, financial, legislative, judicial, or administrative. But in the course of time different groups or committees came to be charged customarily with advice and assistance on particular kinds of matters.

Well before Magna Carta (1215) we find references to 'the one bench or the other.' One bench was the King's Bench, the forerunner of the Court of King's Bench. The other bench was the Common Bench, the forerunner of the Court of Common Pleas.

The King's Bench dealt with *most* matters directly affecting the Crown, including crimes (matters affecting the revenues of the Crown were dealt with by a group which was the forerunner of the Court of the Exchequer). The Common Bench dealt with disputes between subjects. As we should put it today, the

[20] Fortescue, *De Laudibus Legum Angliae*, c. L., p. 116.

King's Bench (and the Exchequer) dealt with public law, and the Common Bench dealt with private law.

That deep-thinking King, Henry II (1154–1189), realized that the peace and prosperity of the realm required that there should be a body of men fitted (*a*) to decide disputes between subjects, and also (*b*) to give adequate counsel to all subjects who had, or thought they had, cause to complain of the conduct of some fellow subject or fellow subjects. To satisfy this requirement he summoned certain men selected with great care from those learned in the law to be serjeants-at-law, — to serve his people, and thereby to serve him.

Of the serjeants-at-law whom he created, the outstanding figure was Ranulph de Glanville (or Glanvil or Glanvill), who was created a serjeant-at-law in 1179, and was in the following year elevated to the position of Chief Justiciar (a person of immense importance and power, — more like a viceroy, or vizier, or prime minister, than those who, in later times, as a consequence of their position as Chief Justice in the King's Bench, were called Lord Chief Justice of England). Glanville efficiently served Henry II as Chief Justiciar throughout the remainder of the reign. He was the first Chief Justiciar who was learned in the law; he was also a mighty man in arms, like some of his predecessors, but he devoted a large amount of his time and efforts to establishing a *national* law to be superior to the local laws which were based upon customs, more often disagreeing than agreeing. He is reputed to have written (about 1181) a treatise on the *Laws and Customs of the Kingdom of England*, which is the earliest treatise on the Common Law which has come down to us. This treatise was highly regarded by Coke, and I believe it may safely be accepted as an accurate statement of the law of that time. The *reliable* history of the Common Law begins with that treatise.

In all probability there was developed in Glanville's time a Common Bench which dealt with disputes between subjects, — nearly all of these disputes relating to rights in real property.

The Common Bench antedated Magna Carta. Coke said: 'At the making of the statute of Magna Carta there were *justiciarii de banco*, which all men confesse to be the court of common pleas.' [21]

In Magna Carta [22] (1215) it was provided: 'Communia placita non sequantur curiam nostram, sed teneantur in aliquo loco

[21] Co. Litt. 71b. [22] Seventeenth clause.

certo.' The subjects complained that the court followed the King about from place to place, wherever he might be from time to time, and they desired that the body dealing with common pleas should thereafter sit in a 'certain place.'

It has been sometimes said that Westminster Hall, which had been known as *the* Aula Regis from the time that William Rufus built the first Westminster Hall, should be such 'certain place.' That is demonstrably not correct. Later sovereigns asserted the right to fix the place wherever they pleased, — provided only that reasonable notice of the place was given to the subjects, and the books show that there were sessions of the court thereafter at various places other than Westminster, including a session at Hertford as late as 1591.[23] But the statement that Westminster Hall was, after Magna Carta, *usually* the 'certain place' is correct.

Later on, both the King's Bench and the Court of Exchequer made very serious encroachments upon the subject-against-subject jurisdiction of the Common Pleas (the detailed examination of the grounds for these encroachments is beyond the scope of this article). But for centuries the Common Pleas was the People's Court.

In Coke's Fourth Institute there is a chapter devoted to the Court of Common Pleas, in which he said:[24]

> This court is the lock and the key of the common law in common pleas, for herein are reall actions, whereupon fines and recoveries (the common assurances of the realm) do passe, and all other reall actions by originall writs are to be determined, and also of all common pleas mixt or personall: in divers of which, as it appeareth before in the chapter of Kings Bench,[25] this court and the kings bench have a concurrent authority. Robert Parning the kings serjeant at law 24 July 14 E. 3. was created chief justice of England, in which office he remained until the 15 · f December following, and then he was made lord treasurer of England; in which office he continued untill the 15 year of E. 3. when he was made lord chancelour of England: and while he was lord chancelour, he would come and sit in this court being the lock and key of the common law, as is aforesaid: and there debate matters in law of greatest difficulty, as it appeareth in the report of the year 17 E. 3. fo. 11. 14. 23. 37. &c. knowing assuredly, that he that knowes not the common law, can never rightly judge of matters in equity.

[23] Capel's Case, 1 Co. Rep. 54a, at 61a. [24] 4th Inst., p. 99.
[25] *Id.*, pp. 70–77.

Beyond question, it was in the Court of Common Pleas that the foundations of the common law as to real property were laid. It has been said by those whose opinions are entitled to credence that some record in the Common Pleas is pertinent to the title of at least half the land in England.

Serjeants-at-law were an integral part of this court. Brian said: '*Un seriaunt est minister de court saunz que le court ne poit eê serue ne occupy.*' [26] They even performed some judicial functions, for example, in the levying of fines.

It was held that even a servant to a serjeant could not be sued in a court other than the Common Pleas, the court quoting a precedent 'where Martyn Serjeant was arrested in London, at the Suit of the Bishop of Winchester, and at the Suit of others, and had a Writ of Priviledge reciting, That Serjeants at the Law were to be attendant to the said Court, ex officio plus quam alibi, and that their service was necessary at this Barre, and therefore commanded them to surcease and to prosecute their Suits in the Common Bench.' [27]

The form of the oath of a serjeant-at-law is enlightening. The oath of, say, a Privy Councillor bound him to serve *the King;* the oath of a King's Serjeant bound him to serve *the King and his people;* the oath of a Brother of the Coif bound him to serve *the King's people.*

> You shall swear well and truly to serve the King's people as one of the serjeants-at-law, and you shall truly counsel them that you be retained with after your cunning; and you shall not defer or delay their causes willingly, for covetness of money, or other thing that may turn you to profit; and you shall give due attendance accordingly. So help you God.

Serjeants-at-law had a right of pre-audience in some other courts (of which much more hereafter), but the bulk of their practice was in the Common Pleas, and in that particular court they had for centuries a monopoly of practice.

This monopoly may have been given in consideration of the following two facts: (1) that they were under a duty to give counsel to *any* subject who came to them for legal aid, regardless of the subject's ability to pay for such counsel; [28] and (2) that by becoming serjeants they were drafted into what may be fairly characterized as the judges-reserve, that the financial

---

[26] Y. B. 11 Edw. IV, Trin. fol. 3b.   [27] Cro. Car. 84 (3 Charles I).

[28] *Paston* v. *Jenney*, Y. B. 11 Edw. IV, Trin. fol. 2b; Viner's Abridgement, Pauper, D; *Doe dem. Bennett* v. *Hale*, 15 Q. B. 171.

emoluments of judges were small,[29] and that it was regarded as only fair, in view of the prospective lean financial future, that they should have a fat financial return in the interval between being created a serjeant-at-law and being made a judge.

There is a record of some 'apprentices' who were summoned to be serjeants-at-law, and who balked until 'persuaded' by Parliament and the imperious Duke of Bedford, who was then Regent, to accept the position.[30] This bears out the thought that highly successful practising barristers were loath to be drafted into the judges-reserve.

It is also to be noted that Coke, who, when still under thirty, won his spurs as junior counsel in the famous case of *Wolfe* v. *Shelley* [31] (a case, be it noted, which was *not* in the Common

---

[29] Speaking of the Justices of the King's Bench and the Common Bench, Coke said (Fourth Institute, p. 100): 'None of them can take any other office, or any fee, or reward but of the king only. And it were behoovefull to the commonwealth and advancement of justice and right, and preferment of well deserving men, if the like course were holden concerning all offices, as well ecclesiasticall as temporall and civill; and that no man following the example of the reverend judges should enjoy two offices. For severall offices were never instituted to be used by any one man.' This restriction, in an age when pluralities were rife, is noteworthy.

Perhaps the judges were entitled to fees, dependent on the amount of business done, in addition to salaries; I regret to state that I have been unable to find satisfactory evidence either way on this. The salaries themselves were certainly small as compared with the income of a successful barrister. In 1279 the yearly salary of the Chief Justice of the Common Pleas was £40, and of the other justices 40 marks. In 1362 the salary of the Chief Justice of the King's Bench was 50 marks, and of the Chief Justice of the Common Pleas was 100 marks. In the first edition of Lord Somers' *Tracts* (vol. II, pp. 23, 24) we find for the year 1617 an item: 'To Sir Edward Coke, Knight, Lord Chief Justice of England, for his fee at 224l. 19s. 9d. by the year and 33l. 6s. 8d. by the Year for his Circuits 258–6–5.' Then the salaries of the other three judges of the King's Bench are given as £188–6–8 apiece, making a total sum by the year of £823–6–5 'besides their yearly Allowances for their Diets in their Circuits.' The salary of Sir Henry Hubberd, Knight, Chief Justice of the Common Pleas, is given at £194–19–9, and of the other three judges at £188–6–8.

These statements surprised me, as I had always supposed that, at the time Coke was 'promoted' from the Chief Justiceship of the Common Pleas to the Chief Justiceship of the King's Bench, the salary of the Chief Justice of the Common Pleas was *greater* (not less) than the salary of the Chief Justice of the King's Bench (note that in 1362 it was double). And Lord Campbell, in his account of the transference of Coke from the Common Pleas to the King's Bench says that Hobart (whose place as Attorney-General Bacon was after) was willing to give up the Attorney-Generalship for the Chief Justiceship of the Common Pleas, but not for the Chief Justiceship of the King's Bench.

Moreover, the date of Coke's dismissal from office has usually been given as 1616 (and not 1617, the date given in Lord Somers' *Tracts*). See Lord Campbell's *Lives of the Chief Justices* (1849 ed.), pp. 276, 292.

But it at least sufficiently appears that Coke's annual salary as a judge was probably less than five per cent of his total annual income from the law during the splendid financial years when he was Attorney-General.

[30] 4 Rot. Parl. 107b.   [31] 1 Co. Rep. 87b.

Pleas, but in the King's Bench), never became a serjeant-at-law until just before his appointment as Chief Justice of the Common Pleas, and that in the heyday of his practice he probably derived an *annual* income from his practice which, considering the value of money in his time, was equivalent to an annual income today of something in the neighborhood of $500,000.[32]

Lord Campbell, in his *Lives of the Chief Justices*, said: 'The Attorney General was supposed to hold by as secure a tenure as a judge;[33] and his fees, particularly from the Court of Wards and Liveries, were enormous, so that he was often unwilling to be "forked up to the bench," which, with a sad defalcation of income, offered him little increase of dignity; for, till the elevation of Jeffreys in the reign of James II, no common-law judge had been made a peer.'[34]

When Mrs. Bardell sued Mr. Pickwick for breach of promise to marry, the action was begun in the Court of Common Pleas. The indignant, worried Mr. Pickwick, momentarily interrupted from his placid observations of life and his kindly but undiscriminating philosophic reflections, sought comfort from his solicitor who soothed him by saying: 'Well, we've done everything that's necessary. I have retained Serjeant Snubbin.'[35]

Came Saint Valentine's Day and the trial. 'Bardell and Pickwick' called the clerk of the court. 'I am for the plaintiff, my Lord,' said Mr. Serjeant Buzfuz. 'Who is with you, Brother Buzfuz?' inquired the Judge.... 'I appear for the defendant, my Lord,' said Mr. Serjeant Snubbin. 'Anybody with you, Brother Snubbin?' inquired the Judge.[36]

[32] The bases for this estimate are as follows: Lord Campbell stated (*Lives*, 1849 ed., p. 267, note) that the emoluments of Coke as Attorney-General were £7,000 a year. To this must be added his income from private practice, for an Attorney-General was at that time (and indeed for a long time thereafter) allowed to continue his private practice, and Coke's income from such practice could scarcely have been less than £3,000. And the value of money at that time was, at least, ten times what it is now.

This estimate is confirmed by the fact that during those years Coke was in receipt of an income so large that he acquired one piece of landed property after another until James I called a halt, saying that he already had as much land as any one subject ought to have. It is also to be noted that Fortescue spoke (see p. 125, *infra*) of £28 a year as the amount necessary for a fashionable young man to spend a year at an Inn of Court, which is certainly not more than one tenth of what it cost in the twentieth century to live at an Inn of Court in style.

[33] Judges held office at the pleasure of the Sovereign until 1701 (12 & 13 Wm. III, c. 2, sec. 3).

[34] Page 266.

[35] *Pickwick Papers*, Chapter XXXI. The *Pickwick Papers* were first printed and issued in monthly parts, the first part in April, 1836, and the last in November, 1837 (with the lapse of one month, June, 1837). [36] *Id.*, Chapter XXXIV.

The judge had, of course, been a serjeant-at-law before he was a judge, and after his elevation to the bench he continued to be a member of the Order of the Coif. Once a serjeant, always a serjeant.[37] So all three of them — the judge, the leader for the plaintiff, and the leader for the defendant — were Brothers.

I recently wrote to Mr. Chief Justice Stone of the Supreme Court of the United States and to Mr. Chief Justice Field of the Supreme Judicial Court of Massachusetts, and each of them authorized me to say that it is not the custom of the court over which he presides that a member of the court should address counsel as 'Brother.'

The relation of practising serjeants-at-law to the judges before whom they practised was unique, — without modern counterpart.

IV. The Relation of the Order of the Coif to the Inns of Court.

The famous four Inns of Court are the Inner Temple, the Middle Temple, Lincoln's Inn, and Gray's Inn. They are unincorporated [38] educational institutions. On important points they closely resemble each other, but each has its own traditions, standards, and modes of conduct, and each has a fascinatingly interesting history, the roots of which are in the remote past, — there were Inns of Court as early as the fourteenth century.

Fortescue was created a serjeant-at-law in 1429, and was later Chief Justice of the King's Bench. He wrote, in Latin, a treatise entitled *De Laudibus Legum Angliae*, which was translated into English and printed long after his death. It contains a chapter [39] largely devoted to the Inns of Court. Whether that chapter was written by Fortescue is doubtful, — it may well be that it is an addition to the original treatise made by some unidentifiable later writer. But it is worth while to give an extract, — it is probably a substantially accurate statement of the facts at a period somewhat subsequent to Fortescue's death.

> That the Method and Form of the Study of the Law may the better appear, I will proceed and describe it to You in the best Manner I can. There belong to it *Ten* lesser Inns, and sometime more, which are called the *Inns of Chancery:* In each of which there are an Hundred Students at the least; and, in some of them, a far

[37] *Sir George Hutchins's Case*, 3 Levinz, 351.

[38] See *The King* v. *The Benchers of Gray's Inn*, 1 Douglas, 353; *The King* v. *The Benchers of Lincoln's Inn*, 4 B. & C. 855.

[39] Chapter XLIX.

greater Number, tho' not constantly residing. The Students are, for the most part, young Men; here they Study the Nature of Original and Judicial Writs, which are the very first Principles of the Law: After they have made some Progress here, and are more advanced in Years, they are admitted into the *Inns of Court*, properly so called: Of these there are Four in Number. In that which is the least frequented, there are about Two hundred Students. In these greater Inns a Student cannot well be maintained under *Eight and twenty Pounds* a Year: And, if He have a Servant to wait on him (as for the most part they have) the Expence is proportionably more: For this Reason, the Students are Sons to Persons of Quality; those of an Inferior Rank not being able to bear the Expences of maintaining and educating their Children in this Way. As to the Merchants, they seldom care to lessen their Stock in Trade by being at such large yearly Expences. So that there is scarce to be found, thro'out the Kingdom, an eminent Lawyer, who is not a Gentleman by Birth and Fortune; consequently they have a greater Regard for their Character and Honour than those who are bred in another Way. There is both in the *Inns of Court*, and the *Inns of Chancery*, a Sort of an *Academy*, or *Gymnasium*, fit for Persons of their Station; where they learn Singing, and all Kinds of Music, Dancing and such other Accomplishments and Diversions (which are called *Revels*) as are suitable to their Quality, and such as are usually practised at Court. At other Times, out of Term, the Greater Part apply themselves to the Study of the Law: Upon Festival Days, and after the Offices of the Church are over, they employ themselves in the Study of Sacred and Prophane History: Here every Thing which is Good and Virtuous is to be learnt: All Vice is discouraged and Banisht. So that Knights, Barons and the Greatest Nobility of the Kingdom, often Place their Children in those Inns of Court; not so much to make the Laws their Study, much less to live by the Profession (having large Patrimonies of their own), but to form their Manners and to preserve them from the Contagion of Vice.... Neither at *Orleans*, where both the *Canon* and *Civil Laws* are professed and studied; and whither Students resort from all Parts; neither at *Angiers*, *Caen*, nor any other University in *France* (*Paris* excepted) are there so many Students, who have past their Minority, as in Our *Inns of Court*, where the Natives only are admitted.

The Inns of Court were fashionable schools for the sons of gentlemen. In a later age, Lord Chesterfield in his letters to his natural son repeatedly emphasized his conviction that the most important part of the education of a young man who might reasonably expect to take a place in affairs was the daily association with persons of quality, with both a social and a cultural background, with whose standards, usages, and modes he should become so familiar that he might look horizontally at them and take his part in their activities with ease, poise, and unaffected pleasure. Probably most of the nobility and gentry who entered their sons in an Inn of Court were influenced by the Chesterfield thought, — the fact that the Inns of Court were schools of manners was even more magnetic than the fact that they were schools of law (although some knowledge of law was fitting for a young man who would probably some day be a magistrate upon a local bench, who might enter Parliament, and who pretty surely would have landed property to protect).[40]

The Revels of the Inns were great society events, not infrequently attended and relished by Royalty. Legend has it that Queen Elizabeth said, on leaving one of these Revels, 'We were much amused.'

But certainly some, and probably a substantial number, of the members of the Inns of Court were dead-in-earnest students of the law who did look forward to a life devoted to the law.

This leads me to speak of the education of Coke. His father, Robert Coke, was a Bencher (see page 129 *infra*) of Lincoln's Inn, and a barrister of extensive practice,[41] with an estate in Norfolk where Edward was born in 1551. His preparatory school was the Grammar School in Norwich. In 1567, he was admitted to Trinity College, Cambridge, and apparently stayed there for four years, although he seems never to have taken a degree, and there is not satisfactory evidence as to just what he did with himself in those four years. If he studied law there, it must have been civil or canon law, for neither Oxford nor Cambridge at that time taught the common law.

In 1571, he entered Clifford's Inn, in London, one of the minor inns (the minor inns, as a group, being called Inns of Chancery), where he stayed a year. In 1572, he entered the Inner Temple, and was there 'called to the Bar' in 1578.

Lord Campbell, in his *Lives of the Chief Justices of England*, said: [42]

> He now steadily persevered in a laborious course, of which, in our degenerate age [the nineteenth century], we can scarcely form a conception. Every morning he rose at three, — in the winter

---

[40] *Paston Letters*, vol. I, p. 58, no. 46.

[41] Stowe's *London*, p. 429. See Johnson, *Life of Sir Edward Coke*, ed. 1837, vol. I, p. 9, note.

[42] Pages 242, 243 (1849 ed.).

season lighting his own fire. He read Bracton, Littleton, the Year Books, and the folio Abridgements of the Law, till the courts met at eight. He then went by water to Westminster, and heard cases argued till twelve, when pleas ceased for dinner. After a short repast in the Inner Temple Hall, he attended 'readings' or lectures in the afternoon, and then resumed his private studies till five, or supper time. This meal being ended, the *moots* took place, when difficult questions of law were proposed and discussed, — if the weather was fine, in the garden by the river side; if it rained, in the covered walks near the Temple Church. Finally, he shut himself up in his chamber, and worked at his common-place book, in which he inserted, under the proper heads, all the legal information he had collected during the day. When nine o'clock struck, he retired to bed, [43] that he might have an equal portion of sleep before and after midnight.

American law schools of today stem from the Inns of Court, the law professors from the 'readers,' and the cases argued by the students (as in the Ames Competition in the Harvard Law School and in similar competitions in many other law schools) from the 'moots.'

Coke himself has given us a terse description of the Inns of Court in his day. He said: [44]

> In the profession of the law, there are Mootemen (which are those that argue readers cases in houses of Chancery, both in terms and grand vacations). Of Mootemen, after eight years study or thereabouts, are chosen Utterbarrister; of these are chosen readers in inns of Chancery: Of Utterbarristers, after they have been of that degree twelve years at least, are chosen Benchers, or Ancients; of which one, that is of the puisne sort, reads yearly in summer vacation, and is called a single Reader; and one of the Ancients that had formerly read, reads in Lent vacat. and is called a Double Reader, and commonly it is between his first and second reading, about nine or ten years. And out of these the King makes choice of his Attorney, and Solicitor General, his Attorney of the Court of Wards and Liveries, and Attorney of the Duchy: and of these Readers, are Serjeants elected by the King, and are, by the King's writ, called *ad statum & gradum servientis ad legem;* and out of these the King electeth one, two, or three as please him, to be his Ser-

---

[43] Throughout his life, Coke kept to the habit of retiring to bed when nine o'clock struck. Shortly after nine one night in 1617, his second wife took advantage of this habit to carry off their daughter in the hope (frustrated) of preventing a marriage of the daughter which Coke had arranged, but to which the mother was bitterly opposed.

[44] Preface to the third part of his *Reports*, pp. xix, xx.

jeants, which are called the King's Serjeants: of Serjeants are by the King also constituted the honourable and reverend Judges, and sages of the law. For the young student, which most commonly cometh from one of the universities, for his entrance or beginning were first instituted, and erected eight Houses of Chancery, to learn there the elements of the law, that is to say, Clifford's-inn, Lyon's-inn, Clement's-inn, Barnard's-inn, Staple's-inn, Furnival's-inn, Thavie's-inn, and New-inn; and each of these houses consist of forty or thereabouts: for the Readers, Utterbarristers, Mootemen, and inferior Students, are 4 famous and renowned Colleges, or Houses of Court, called The Inner Temple, to which the first three Houses of Chanc. appertain; Gray's-Inn, to which the next two belong; Lincoln's-Inn, which enjoyeth the last two but one; and the Middle Temple, which hath only the last: each of the Houses of Court consists of Readers above twenty; of Utterbarristers above thrice so many; of young Gentlemen about the number of eight or nine score, who there spend their time in study of law, and in commendable exercises fit for gentlemen: the Judges of the law and Serjeants being commonly above the number of 20, are equally distinguished into two higher and more eminent Houses, called Serjeants' Inn:

We see then that, even if the preliminary training in an Inn of Chancery be disregarded, there were four grades, culminating in the grade of serjeant-at-law:

(1) A period of study as students (using that term in its modern sense). This period was a very long period, according to modern standards. Coke himself was 'called to the Bar' after six years' study in the Inner Temple, but that was a tribute to his extraordinary ability and intensity of application, for he tells us that the usual period was eight years. He called the students 'mootmen.' They were also sometimes called 'apprentices below the Bar' (here 'apprentices' was used in its primary sense of persons who were learning, but who were not yet learned); and they were also sometimes called 'inner barristers,' — a name probably given to them because they sat on the forms or benches nearest to the disputants at the arguments of moots. In these arguments the usual procedure seems to have been that there should be four disputants, — two 'inner barristers' and two 'utter barristers.'

(2) Then those who had proved themselves fit were 'called to the Bar.' The number called was very small according to modern standards. Of course this was only an expression of opinion by those in whom the powers of a particular Inn of Court were

vested that the persons, so called, were qualified *to begin some kinds of practice*. But the judges came to accept that call, without more, as satisfactory evidence of qualification to begin the practice of the law.

The persons who were so 'called' were spoken of as 'apprentices at the Bar' (a *learned* apprentice was *not* regarded as a contradiction in terms) and were also spoken of as 'utter (or outer) barristers,' — a name probably given to them because they sat on the forms or benches farthest away from the disputants at the argument of moots, and to contrast them with 'inner barristers.'

(3) After twelve years more, spent as 'apprentices at the Bar' or 'utter barristers,' they became *eligible* to be selected as 'benchers,' or 'antients,' the body in which was vested the powers of the Inn. And from the 'benchers,' or 'antients,' were selected the readers.

(4) From those who had acquitted themselves particularly well as 'apprentices at the Bar' or 'utter barristers' (usually, but not always, persons who had been readers) were selected those who were to be advanced to the very top of the Bar as serjeants-at-law.

A long, very long, evolution of those fittest to serve the King's people in the law. The general idea was that the serjeants-at-law, the lawyers *par excellence*, were to be few, very few; but that they were to be good, very good.

And for centuries the serjeants-at-law were very good indeed. They played a vital part in moulding the common law, — a part which was in some ways quite as important, productive, and indispensable as the work of the judges themselves.

The whole system stems back to the general idea of Henry II. The Bar was made for the nation, and not the nation for the Bar. The lawyers must serve the King's subjects.

It sometimes happened that a writ of summons to be a serjeant-at-law was issued to an apprentice at the Bar, or utter barrister, who was not a bencher. In such case the person summoned forthwith took his place on the bench of the Inn, but his life as a bencher was very short, — confined to the interval between the receipt of the writ and his taking the oath as a serjeant-at-law.

Any bencher of an Inn of Court, on being sworn as a serjeant-at-law, ceased to be a member of his Inn of Court. There was a ceremony by which he was 'rung out by the chapel bell.' He forthwith became a member of Serjeants' Inn, but he often returned as an honored guest to his old Inn.

The Serjeants' Inn [45] was the place where the Brothers of the Coif, whether judges or practising serjeants-at-law, kept a commons, and lodged when they pleased, — usually during term time. The two most famous Serjeants' Inns were the one located in Fleet Street, which was given up in the middle of the eighteenth century, and the one in Chancery Lane, which was pulled down in 1877.

A Serjeants' Inn was like an exclusive club, the membership being restricted to Brothers of the Coif. There the Brothers who were judges and the Brothers who were practising serjeants-at-law ate, drank, and talked together as fellow clubmates.

V. The Relation of the Order of the Coif to Saint Paul's Cathedral.

At one time in Normandy courts of law were held in the Cathedral at Rouen. Similarly, Saint Paul's Cathedral in London was used as a meeting place for serjeants-at-law and their clients. Thus Fortescue said, [46] 'The *Judges of England* do not sit in the King's Courts above three Hours in the Day, that is, from Eight in the Morning till Eleven. The Courts are not open in the Afternoon. The Suitors of the Court betake themselves to the *Pervise*, and other Places, to advise with the Serjeants at Law, and other their Counsel, about their Affairs.' And Dugdale said [47] that at Saint Paul's 'Each Lawyer and Serjeant, at his Pillar heard his Client's Cause, and took notes thereof upon his knee. . . . After the Serjeants feast ended [see page 134, *infra*], they do still go to *Pauls* in their Habits, and there choose their Pillar, whereat to hear their Clyents cause (if any come) in memory of that old Custome.'

There is a striking resemblance between lawyers in the Roman Forum and lawyers in Saint Paul's Cathedral. The Cathedral was, so to speak, offices for serjeants-at-law, where clients could seek them, — the busiest time probably being in the afternoon when the courts had risen and the midday meal was finished.

At the present day, English barristers have no clients except solicitors. A modern Shakespeare might say: 'The solicitor that doth hedge a barrister.' A person who needs legal advice must not go to a barrister, he must go to a solicitor, and the solicitor

---

[45] There was a 'Le Sergeantes Inne' at least as early as 1544.

[46] *De Laudibus Legum Angliae*, c. LI, p. 120.

[47] *Origines Juridiciales*, c. LV, p. 142a.

then retains and 'instructs' a barrister. For a person who needs legal advice to go direct to a barrister is one of those things that just 'is not done,' and the mere suggestion of such a procedure will cause eyebrows and even hands to be raised in astonishment.

But this is a rule of legal etiquette; it is *not* a rule of law.[48] And it is only a *modern* rule of etiquette. For centuries there was no such rule of etiquette even with respect to the serjeants-at-law, who were at the very top of the English Bar. They were created that they might *serve the King's people*, and they swore that they would do so. It was of the essence that they should be accessible, and for centuries they *were* accessible in a way that the present-day King's Counsel definitely are not.

I was interested to see what mentions of serjeants-at-law were made by the author of the *Vision of Piers the Plowman*, or Chaucer, or Shakespeare. I found no reference in Shakespeare. There were two mentions of serjeants-at-law in the *Vision of Piers the Plowman*, and these have been given above (page 116). And there is a passage in Chaucer's Prologue to the *Canterbury Tales* which deserves to be given in full.

Chaucer wrote in the last half of the fourteenth century. It has been said that he had in his youth been a student in the Inner Temple, and that on one occasion 'Geffrye Chaucer was fined two shillinges for beatinge a Franciscane Fryer in fletestreat.'

The passage is as follows:

> A Sergeant of the Lawe, war and wys,
> That often hadde been at the Parvys,
> Ther was also, ful riche of excellence.
> Discreet he was and of greet reverence —
> He semed swich, his wordes weren so wise.
> Justice he was ful often in assise,
> By patente and by pleyn commissioun,
> For his science and for his heigh renoun;
> Of fees and robes hadde he many oon.
> So greet a purchasour was nowher noon.
> Al was fee simple to hym in effect;
> His purchasyng myghte nat been infect.
> Nowher so bisy a man as he ther nas,
> And yet he semed bisier than he was.

[48] *Doe dem. Bennett* v. *Hale*, 15 Q.B. 171.

In termes hadde he caas and doomes alle
That from the tyme of kyng William were falle.
Therto he koude endite, and make a thyng,
Ther koude no wight pynche at his writyng;
And every statut koude he pleyn by rote.
He rood but hoomly in a medlee cote,
Girt with a ceint of silk, with barres smale;
Of his array telle I no lenger tale.[49]

As to the part which a serjeant-at-law played in riding the circuit ('Justice he was ful often in assise, by patente and by pleyn commissioun') see page 110, *supra*. As to the many robes which a serjeant-at-law had, see page 113, *infra*.

There has been much dispute over the scope of 'parvys.' The word was, no doubt, sometimes used to apply only to the *porch* of a church. But there is evidence which justifies the conclusion that the pillars to which the serjeants-at-law were allotted included pillars in the nave. Note that there are references in literature to 'Paul's Walk,' a fashionable promenade or rendezvous, and this seems certainly to have included the nave of the Cathedral. Probably (but not surely) 'parvys' as used by Chaucer included the nave as well as the porch.

VI. The Selection of Serjeants-at-law and the Ceremonies Incident to their Creation.

Fortescue said that the Chief Justice of the Common Pleas, by and with the consent of all the judges, is wont to pitch upon, as often as he sees fitting, seven or eight of the discreeter persons, such as have made the greatest proficiency in the general study of the laws and whom they judge best qualified. The manner is, to deliver their names in writing to the Lord High Chancellor of England; who, in virtue of the King's Writ, shall forthwith command every one of the persons so pitched upon, that he be before the King, at a day certain, to take upon him the state and degree of a serjeant-at-law, under a great penalty, in every one of the said Writs specified and limited.[50]

For centuries, it was not regarded as proper in any wise to press for, or solicit, such an appointment. But in later days such solicitations were made.

The creation of serjeants-at-law was treated as a matter of

---

[49] Prologue to the *Canterbury Tales*, lines 309–330, as edited by Robinson.
[50] *De Laudibus Legum Angliae*, c. L, pp. 113, 114.

great solemnity, and the ceremonies were elaborate. They have been spoken of as rivalling the ceremonies attendant upon a coronation.

'*Serviens ad legem est nosme de dignitie, come cheualer et est un degree.*' [51]

Dugdale gives in great detail the ceremonies incident to the creation of seven serjeants-at-law in 1555.[52]

First, they chose a draper to furnish them with cloth. Each serjeant had robes of scarlet, of violet in grayn, of brown blew, and of mustard and Murrey, five and a half yards to each robe. Each serjeant also had eight liveries for eight servants, of mustard and Murrey cloth, one and a half yards to each livery, and nearly one hundred other liveries. Liveries given on such an occasion were excepted in the statutes restricting the use of liveries.[53] The custom of giving liveries lasted into the eighteenth century.

Next, they chose a goldsmith to make their rings of gold. Rings of the finest angel gold were given to Philip and Mary, the King and Queen, and rings of gold were also given to over fifty other persons, including the Lord Chancellor, the Lord Steward, the Lord Treasurer of England, the Lord Privy Seal, the Lord Chamberlain of England, the Justices of the King's Bench, the Justices of the Common Pleas, the Barons of the Exchequer, the Master of the Rolls, four of the antientest serjeants, the King's Attorney-General, and the King's Solicitor-General. Each serjeant made choice of a person or persons to see to the disposing of the rings.

They also appointed persons to serve during the time of the feast, including a steward and a comptroller.

The *Steward* and *Comptroller* beforementioned, in the morning that the new elected Serjeants had taken their coifes, and ended Breakfast in the Hall, went before them, bearing White staves, till they came without the Temple-gate into *Fleetstreet:* which done they made their return into the Inner-Temple, to manage things decent and convenient in the Hall, for the Feast.

The Serjeants being returned from *Westminster* Hall to the Inner-Temple, and the Judges and great men being assembled to participate of the Feast, the said *Steward* and *Comptroller* went before the first course, to the Lords Table. Which being performed, and the Lords placed, they kept order in the Hall till Dinner ended.

---

[51] Brooke's *Abridgement*, nosme de dignitie.

[52] *Origines Juridiciales*, c. XLVIII.   [53] See 8 Edw. IV, c. 2.

After the Feast, and Tables voided, the said Officer went before the new elected Serjeants from the Temple-Hall, attending upon them thence, with white staves bare-headed, through *Fleetstreet*, with many others accompanying them unto *St. Thomas of Acres* in London, and thence to the Cathedral Church of St. *Paul;* and after some accustomed Ceremonies performed in both places, they returned unto *Serjeants Inne* in *Fleetstreet*, where they received thanks of the said Serjeants, and either of them a Ring of Gold: and so with Congees and reverence on both parties, departed, and were dismissed.

There came from every Inne of Court eight of the chiefest gentlemen Students there, to be Servitors in the Hall during the Feast.

Also to every several Serjeant was allowed from the Inne of Court, whereof he was a Fellow, three Gentlemen of his choosing; the one to attend him at the Table for Sewer, another for Carver, and the third for his Cupbearer.

The Lords of the Councell, and Peers; the Lord Mayor and Aldermen of London, the Judges, the old Serjeants; the *King's Attorney*, and *Sollicitor* general; the Chancellour of the Exchequer; the *King's Attorney of the Court of Wards* and *Dutchy*, Sir *Edw. Montagu* and Sir *Roger Cholmley*, were all of them invited to the Feast, by *Steward* and *Comptroller*, whose office it was to invite persons of State.

Also the new elected Serjeants sate all Dinner time, on the Bench side, distinct one from another a good space; and had their Table on the worthiest side of the Hall, and every one a whole mess, served out in Lordly state.

There was one table prepared for the Lords of the King's and Queen's Privy Council and certain Spanish grandees.

Dugdale does not say that either King Philip or Queen Mary came to the feast, but on a previous similar occasion both King Henry VIII and Queen Catherine attended at the feast (although in separate chambers).

The dishes at the feast included 'Boyled capons in Whitebroth, Swans rosted, Bustards, Chewet pies, Pikes, Capons rosted, Venison pasties, Hern and Bittern, Pheasants rosted, custards, jellyes, Cranes, Partridges, Red Deer, Sturgeon, Woodcocks, Plovers, Quince-Pies, Rabbet Suckers, Snipes rosted, Larkes, March-panes.'

Dugdale gives no inventory of the potables. But he does give two straws of information, — one of the new serjeants contributed a hogshead of claret, and another 'half a Tun of claret.'

It also appears that the new serjeants entertained guests invited to dine with them privately. They were expected, *pro hac vice*, to play the rôle of Santa Claus. I do not see how, taking everything into account, any serjeant could have made a total expenditure of less than two or three hundred pounds, — a very considerable sum of money in 1555.

It was the custom for the serjeant-designate to appoint some good friend to present the rings in his behalf. Such friend was in Coke's day known as his 'pony,' — North (afterward Lord Keeper Guilford) was Coke's 'pony.' Later,[54] such friend was called his 'colt.' [55]

[54] Wynne's *Miscellany*, p. 333; *Memorials of Mr. Serjeant Bellasis*, 1893 ed., p. 11.

[55] I was curious to learn (or guess) the origin of the use of the words 'pony' and 'colt' in such a connection.

In Doctor Heylin's *Voyage to France* he said, in speaking of the University of Orleans: 'In the bestowing of their degrees here they are very liberal, and deny no man that is able to pay his fees. *Legem ponere* is with them more powerful than *legem dicere*; and he that hath but his gold ready, shall have a sooner despatch than the best scholar upon the ticket.'

Now, the rings, including the massive ring presented to the Sovereign (Mr. Serjeant Bellasis presented Queen Victoria with a ring 'massive enough to cover two joints of the finger') may have been regarded as in the nature of a fee for the degree of Serjeant-at-Law.

In the sixteenth century, '*legem pone*' had come to be slang for gold and silver coins, — 'hard cash.' Thus, in Thomas Tusser's *Five Hundred Points of Good Husbandrie*, edition of 1580, collated with the editions of 1573 and 1577 (published in 1878 for the English Dialect Society), in the tenth chapter, entitled 'Good husbandlie lessons worthie to be followed by such as will thrive,' the first two lines of verse 29 were:

'Use (*legem pone*) to paie at thy daie,
But vse not (*Oremus*) for often delaie.'

And, in America today, it is not uncommon for a creditor to demand that his debtor 'pony up.'

It may also be noted that in England 'pony' became slang for a definite amount of hard cash, — to wit, twenty-five pounds (Murray's *New English Dictionary*), and it may well be that that would be not far from the average amount paid in medieval days for the rings. Fortescue (chap. L, p. 114) said that his rings cost him fifty pounds, and he obviously considered that he had been lavish. (It is to be remembered that the value of money today is only a small fraction of what it was in medieval times; see page 123, *supra*).

In 1 Modern, Case 30 (Mich.), we find this memorandum: 'Seventeen Serjeants being made the 14th day of *November*, a day or two after SERJEANT POWIS, the junior of them all, coming to the king's bench bar, LORD CHIEF JUSTICE KELYNGE told him, that he had something to say to him, *viz.* that the rings which he and the rest of the Serjeants had given weighed but *eighteen shillings* a-piece; whereas FORTESCUE, in his book *De Laudibus Legum Angliae*, says, "THE RINGS given to THE CHIEF JUSTICES and to THE CHIEF BARON ought to weigh *twenty shillings* a-piece"; and that he spoke not this expecting a recompence, but that it might not be drawn into a precedent, and that the young gentlemen there might take notice of it.'

If the rings were the 'pone,' it is easy to understand how the term came to be applied not only to the thing given, but also to the person who gave the thing.

(1) '*Legem ponere*' was shortened to '*Legem pone*'; then (2) the '*legem*' was cut out; then (3) the spelling was changed from 'pone' to 'pony'; and then (4) 'pony' came

To solemnize the proceedings there were addresses to the new serjeants, and all of those which have come down to us show how vital to the welfare of the nation the maintenance of the high standards of this Ancient and Honourable Brotherhood was regarded.

The *gradus* of a serjeant-at-law gave social, as well as legal, precedence. A serjeant-at-law had social precedence just below a Knight Bachelor, and above a Companion of the Bath or an admiral or a general. And what is more — and this is very important — the wife of a serjeant-at-law took social precedence, in the meticulously regulated English social hierarchy, according to the rank of her husband, although the wife of a bishop, or even a privy councillor, did not have a social precedence similar to that of her husband.

VII. The Decline and Fall of the Order of the Coif.

The decline began in the Tudor days with (1) an appointment of an '*in uno saltu*' serjeant-at-law and judge; and (2) the giving of the title of 'Queen's Counsel Extraordinary' to Bacon.

(1) In 1545, Henry VIII desired to make a judge out of a person who was not a serjeant-at-law. He respected the form, but disregarded the substance, of the usage which had been maintained for centuries, that such a judge should be selected from the serjeants-at-law. He summoned him as a serjeant-at-law, and forthwith, upon the completion of the formalities of his creation, raised him to the bench.[56]

This precedent was thereafter repeatedly followed. The serjeant-at-law requisite for judicial appointments became a mere form. Indeed, at a later time, a statute was passed changing the rule that a serjeant-at-law could not be created in Vaca-

to be applied to the person who gave the rings in behalf of the serjeant-designate.

But why was 'colt' used later in the place of 'pony'? On this, I have nothing to offer better than a hunch.

The word 'pony,' in horsey language, means a small horse, — for example, a Shetland pony. Ponies were fitting playthings for children. But the English spoke (and for that matter, still speak) of the blooded, male, entire three-year-olds who race in the Derby and other races as 'colts.'

It is possible that some of those (and their name was legion) who had not the slightest idea why 'pony' was used to characterize a person who took a part in that gorgeous, awe-inspiring spectacle, the creation of a serjeant-at-law, thought it fitting that, if horsey language was to be used at all, the term used should arouse associations with the Sport of Kings, and not with the sport of children.

Sed quaere. Slang moves in undetectable ways its vocabulary to achieve.

[56] Holdsworth, *History of English Law*, 1937 ed., vol. V, p. 341.

tion so as to make the '*in uno saltu*' performance stageable at any time.[57]

In the nineteenth century the necessity for the form was abolished (1875).[58] But the substance had long since gone. For example: In the years 1800 to 1875, both inclusive, seventy-four persons were made a Chief Justice or other Justice of the King's Bench, or a Chief Justice or other Justice of the Common Pleas, or a Chief Baron of the Exchequer. Of these, fifty-seven (all but seventeen) were summoned to be serjeants-at-law in the same year that they were placed on the bench. The seventeen practising serjeants-at-law raised to the bench were: Archibald, Bayley, Best, Bosanquet, Byles, Coleridge, Cockburn, Copley (Lord Lyndhurst), Crowder, Dallas, Erle, Laurence, Richards, Shee, Talfourd, Thomason, and Wilde (Lord Truro). The average ability of the seventeen, as evidenced by their opinions, was, it is submitted, above the average ability of the fifty-seven.

Before we leave this topic, it may be noted that Coke himself was an '*in uno saltu*' serjeant-at-law and judge. That puzzled me when I first discovered it, but the explanation now seems clear.

He was called to the Bar at the Inner Temple in 1578. He was not eligible to be made a bencher until he had been an 'apprentice at the Bar' or 'utter barrister' for twelve years. Now, in 1590 he was made a bencher and in 1592 was made a reader, and he gave some lectures on the Statute of Uses; he was just the kind of person whom one would expect soon to be summoned to take the *gradum* of a serjeant-at-law.

But by his great abilities he had attracted the attention of Burleigh, that most efficient scout for Elizabeth, and in 1592, at the age of forty-one, he was made Solicitor-General, and two years later was made Attorney-General. His conduct of trials as the prosecuting officer has been subjected to severe adverse criticism (in which, despite my profound admiration for Coke, I concur); but his conduct seems to have suited Elizabeth and she kept him where he was until her death. And no serjeant-at-law could (without losing his *gradum* as such) be made Solicitor-General or Attorney-General.

How Coke himself felt about that is a matter of conjecture, but I surmise that he was well content. It has been charged that Coke *worshipped* the Almighty Pound. I do not think that that

[57] 39 Geo. III, c. 113.

[58] 36 & 37 Vict., c. 66, sec. 8, the operative date of which became November 1, 1875.

charge is justified. He certainly proved himself to be more interested in preserving the liberties of the subjects against the
usurpations of James I than he was in making money; by his
public services, particularly with reference to the so-called Peti-
tion of Right, he paved the way for the resistance to attempts
at monarchical domination which at long last resulted in the
'Glorious Revolution' of 1688.

But the lack of money is the root of many anxieties, and Coke
unquestionably had a money-making stage in his life. I have no
doubt that he thoroughly enjoyed those years as Attorney-
General when the golden flood (at a rate equivalent to five hundred thousand dollars a year at the present time, — see page
123, *supra*) flowed into his bank account and flowed out again
into land. One is reminded of Chaucer's line, descriptive of a
serjeant-at-law.[59]

James I kept Coke as Attorney-General from 1603, the date
of his accession, to 1606, when he made him Chief Justice of the
Common Pleas. James followed the Tudor precedent of observ-
ing the form of the ancient rule, and Coke was therefore one of
the '*in uno saltu*' serjeants-at-law and judges.

Before we leave Coke, it is worth while to note how different
were the circumstances in which he was made Chief Justice of
the Common Pleas from the circumstances in which he was in
1613 made Chief Justice of the King's Bench. Possibly his elevation to be Chief Justice of the Common Pleas was the result
of some Bacon intrigue, but I incline to think that it was not.
There is no question but that James I admired Coke's abilities
and was anxious to have his support, and he probably regarded
the appointment as a friendly act, which might safely be made
(for all judges held at that time at the King's pleasure),[60] and
which he hoped would incline that very influential person in
legal matters to make decisions which would please him (he
was later disillusioned). And I surmise that Coke was content
with the wealth that he had accumulated and was glad to have
a new world to conquer. But the 'elevation' to be the Chief
Justice of the King's Bench is a different story. Bacon, the

---

[59] 'So greet a purchasour was nowher noon.' Prologue to *Canterbury Tales*, line 318;
see page 131, *supra*.

[60] So far as I know, the only judge who, prior to 1701 (the date of the enactment of
12 & 13 Will. III, c. 2, sec. 3), held during good behavior was Chief Baron Walter who
had received a patent, 1 Charles I, *quamdiu se bene gesserit*. See Cro. Car. 203, memorandum. All other judges held *durante bene placito regis*.

'wisest, brightest, meanest of mankind,'[61] hankered after the Attorney-Generalship and Hobart, the Attorney-General, was ready to quit, if he were made Chief Justice of the Common Pleas, but not if he were made Chief Justice of the King's Bench, the financial emoluments of which office were probably a good deal less than those of the office of Chief Justice of the Common Pleas; so Coke 'was kicked upstairs' into the King's Bench, to make room for Hobart, who in turn made room for Bacon.

(2) To return from this digression as to Coke to the second fact in the Tudor days which was handwriting on the wall for the Order of the Coif. Bacon was a nephew of Burleigh and therefore a person whom Elizabeth was inclined to indulge (if it did not cost too much). He induced her to make him 'Queen's Counsel Extraordinary.' Her Queen's Serjeants were her Counsel *in Ordinary*; Bacon became the first person to rejoice in the resounding title 'Queen's Counsel *Extraordinary*.'

What Bacon obtained from the appointment other than a resounding title was probably nil. There is no record that Elizabeth gave him a patent, or a salary, or that she assigned him any specific duties to perform. But Bacon seems to have been able to convey to James I a distorted conception of what Elizabeth had done and to induce him to follow his cousin's 'precedent,' and to make him 'King's Counsel Extraordinary,' and to give him both a patent and a pension.

The matter might, perhaps, have passed into history with only the significance of a flamboyant Baconian episode. But it was a magnetic precedent, and it was later followed, at first in only a few cases, but later on in rapidly swelling numbers.

The struggle to be at the top of the English Bar, to have place and precedence, has been fierce, — jungle fierce. The King's (or Queen's) Counsel ultimately succeeded in reducing the serjeants-at-law to a rank in court (although not in society) inferior to the rank of King's (or Queen's) Counsel. This came about in the following way:

The King's (or Queen's) Counsel *in Ordinary* had for centuries been the King's (or Queen's) Serjeants-at-Law.[62] As such, they had been the leaders of the English Bar, and, in comparison to them, even the Attorney-General and Solicitor-General were inferior Crown officers. They had, even when not acting for the

[61] Pope, *Essay on Man*, Epistle IV, line 282.
[62] See page, 110 *supra*.

Crown, the right of pre-audience in all common-law courts over other serjeants-at-law. In a word, the *Serviens Regis ad legem* ranked above the *Serviens ad legem* (see page 110, *supra*).

In the patent which James I gave to Bacon as 'King's Counsel Extraordinary' it was stated that he was given 'place and precedence in our courts.'

Now, the James I precedent was followed in the patents later issued to other King's (or Queen's) Counsel 'Extraordinary.' If nobody had been made King's (or Queen's) Counsel 'Extraordinary,' unless he really were to be employed to aid, as special counsel, the Crown's legal advisers in Ordinary, the number so appointed would have been small, and the position of the serjeants-at-law would, to be sure, have been damaged, but the damage would not have been devastating.

But — and here's the point — in the course of the nineteenth century the number of King's (or Queen's) Counsel 'Extraordinary' became very large, and there was no pretense even of limiting the number to those who were to be special counsel to the Sovereign. Indeed, the adjective 'Extraordinary' fell into disuse; everybody knew that the persons so appointed were only in name counsel to the Sovereign. Worse still, it seems to me pretty plain (although no doubt the soundness of my criticism may be challenged) that in some (by no means all) of the cases where such appointments were made, the appointments were not based solely on the outstanding ability which the barrister so honored had demonstrated in practice at the Bar, but that 'Influence' came to play its sapping, undermining part.

In 1765, there were nine serjeants 'who constantly attend.' [63] In 1790, the earliest Law List in the Harvard Law Library (the Law Lists do, in fact, go back to 1775) gives twenty-one King's Counsel, and twelve serjeants-at-law. Eldon was inclined to think that the total number of King's Counsel should not exceed twenty. But the number grew and grew. In 1875 (the last year in which serjeants-at-law were created), the Law List gives one hundred and eighty-four Queen's Counsel and eighteen practising serjeants-at-law.

'Place and precedence in our courts' put the most junior of King's (or Queen's) Counsel ahead of the most ancient of the serjeants-at-law.

Now what did 'place and precedence' amount to? Did it merely amount to a right to the best places at the tables provided

[63] Wynne, *Miscellany*, p. 382.

for the convenience of counsel? It amounted to a great deal more than that. It amounted to a right of pre-audience.

A right of pre-audience strikes an American lawyer of today as all wrong. We are accustomed to have the calendars of courts arranged by the clerks of the courts in the chronological order of papers received, unaffected by the personality of counsel; the clerk of a court in making up a calendar is supposed to be no respecter of persons.

But the old English system was altogether different. For example: In the King's Bench the serjeants-at-law did not have a monopoly (note that if they had had a monopoly there, Coke could not have argued in *Wolfe* v. *Shelley*),[64] but they did have a right of pre-audience. The serjeants-at-law were entitled to be heard before all other counsel (the serjeants-at-law, as between themselves, being entitled to be heard according to seniority). This put the clients of advocates other than serjeants-at-law at a great disadvantage.

It was at one time the rule that the senior serjeant-at-law would be heard in the King's Bench on all the motions in *all* the causes on which he had been retained, before the serjeant-at-law ranking next in order of seniority was heard on all the motions in *all* the causes in which he had been retained, and so on and on until all serjeants-at-law had been heard. Meanwhile, other counsel were cooling their heels. Lord Mansfield partially remedied this by ruling that no counsel should be heard on a second motion until all counsel who desired to be heard (whether serjeants-at-law or not) had been heard on one motion.[65]

But this was a palliation, not a cure, and one can readily understand how eager were counsel who were not serjeants-at-law to change this state of affairs.

If they had sought to abolish all right of pre-audience *based on the personality of counsel*, an American lawyer of today would be heartily in sympathy with them. But that was not what they were after. They did not seek to abolish the right of pre-audience based on the personality of counsel. No, indeed. They wished that retained. What they wanted, and what they obtained, was the right of pre-audience for *themselves*.

They completely turned the tables on the serjeants-at-law. It was now for serjeants-at-law to cool their heels while King's (or Queen's) Counsel had the ear of the court.

The thin edge of the Baconian wedge was driven home and

[64] See page 122, *supra*.   [65] See 1 Burrow's Reports, 57.

smashed to smithereens the advantages of serjeants-at-law in the common-law courts other than the Common Pleas.

Was that for better or for worse? The coif was the emblem of the serjeants-at-law; the silk gown is the emblem of King's (or Queen's) Counsel. Was it better or worse for the nation that, where there had once been one silk coif, there were now ten silk gowns?

In the Common Pleas, the court with which from time immemorial the serjeants-at-law had been most closely connected,[66] they made their last stand.

In the period after the enactment of the Reform Bill in 1832 (a period of extensive legal reforms), there were those who decried and denounced the Order of the Coif as an outmoded, medieval institution, which was no longer fit to survive. It may be noted in contrast that Cromwell had no quarrel with the Order of the Coif, that he made Maynard the Lord Protector's Serjeant (page 110, *supra*), that he made several persons (including Hale) serjeants-at-law, and that he seems always to have followed the usages existing when he acquired control of the nation.

In 1834, William IV issued a Royal Mandate assuming to abolish the exclusive right of the serjeants-at-law to be heard at the bar of the Common Pleas. It has been said that this was done at the instigation of Campbell, the Attorney-General.

Certain serjeants-at-law brought a proceeding (heard in 1839 by the Judicial Committee of the Privy Council) to test the validity of this Royal Mandate. Campbell, who was still Attorney-General, submitted that it was not the function of the Judicial Committee to advise the Crown on such a matter. But he proceeded to say, probably to the amazement of those present: 'But if you are to give any opinion or advice to Her Majesty, I apprehend it will be this, that the matter rests entirely with the judges of the Common Pleas, who have the power to regulate who shall practise in the Court. . . . I am bound to state fairly the opinion to which I have come, and it is this, that this was not binding upon the Court of Common Pleas, that the Chief-Justice and the other judges of the Court were not at all bound to act upon it.'[67]

The Judicial Committee gave no judgment,[68] in this respect

---

[66] See pp. 118–124, *supra*.   [67] Manning, *Serviens ad Legem*, p. 119.
[68] *Id.*, at p. 155.

following the suggestion of the Attorney-General. But, as the Attorney-General had himself, so to speak, repudiated his reputed child, the result was a victory for the serjeants-at-law.

This victory, however, was short-lived. In 1846, Parliament passed a statute [69] which provided:

> Whereas it would tend to the more equal Distribution and to the consequent Despatch of Business in the Superior Courts of Common Law at *Westminster*, and would at the same Time be greatly for the Benefit of the Public, if the Right of Barristers at Law to practise, plead, and to be heard extended equally to all the said Courts; but by reason of the exclusive Privilege of Serjeants at Law to practise, plead, and have Audience in the Court of Common Pleas at *Westminster* during Term Time, such Object cannot be effected without the Authority of Parliament: Be it therefore enacted ... That from and after the passing of this Act all Barristers at Law, according to their respective Rank and Seniority, shall and may have and exercise equal Rights and Privilege of practising, pleading, and Audience in the said Court of Common Pleas at *Westminster* with the said Serjeants at Law. ...

Queen's Counsel to the right of them; the Statute of 1846 to the left of them. The serjeants-at-law were doomed.

The *coup de grâce* was given in 1875 by the statute [70] which abolished the necessity of even going through the form of making a person a serjeant-at-law before he was made a judge. No serjeant-at-law was created after 1875. In 1877, Serjeants' Inn was pulled down. The Order lived on in name until all persons who were serjeants-at-law in 1875 had died. With the death of Lord Lindley, who died in 1921 at the age of ninety-three, the English Order of the Coif became extinct.

Serjeants-at-law in Ireland are beyond the scope of this article. It is not many years ago that one of the passengers on an ocean liner plying from the United States to England was a very virile person, — Mr. Serjeant Sullivan of Hibernia. I hope he is still alive.

A few words as to some of the minor aspects of the decline and fall.

(*a*) In 1623, an Order in Council gave precedence to the Attorney-General and Solicitor-General above all the King's Serjeants, 'except the two ancientist.' In 1814, an Order of the

[69] 9 & 10 Vict., c. 54.

[70] 36 & 37 Vict., c. 66, sec. 8. As to operative date, see 37 & 38 Vict., c. 83, sec. 2.

Prince Regent gave precedence to the Attorney-General and Solicitor-General over all King's Serjeants, without any exception. For the first time, the Attorney-General became the titular head of the English Bar.

(*b*) King's (or Queen's) Counsel 'Extraordinary' upon their appointment asserted the right forthwith to take their place as a bencher of the Inn of Court to which they belonged. The number of benchers became swollen to an embarrassing, unwieldy number.

(*c*) The old Cathedral of Saint Paul's was burnt in the great fire in 1666. The custom of allotting pillars to new serjeants-at-law seems to have perished with it.

(*d*) Lucullan feasts fell out of fashion, and there seem to have been none after the middle of the eighteenth century. The custom of giving rings lasted to the end, although the number was much reduced. The custom of wearing particolored robes passed away at a relatively early date (Coke balked at wearing a particolored robe on his creation as a serjeant-at-law and was excused), but even after 1875 most, if not all, of the surviving serjeants-at-law wore, on stately occasions, gorgeous scarlet robes.[71]

That's the tale. And what is the moral of the tale? Let each deep-thinking reader ponder these things in his heart and draw his own moral. I venture to prophesy that there will be as many differing morals drawn as there be differing philosophies of life.

In closing, I wish to express my thanks for the very valuable assistance given to me on various points in the article by Professors Fred N. Robinson, Bartlett J. Whiting, and F. W. C. Hersey, of the English Department; by Professor Harold H. Burbank, of the Economics Department; by Professor Eldon James, Harvard Law Librarian; by Mr. Robert H. Haynes, Assistant Librarian at the Widener Library; and by Mr. George L. Haskins, son of the late Professor Charles H. Haskins, who is following in his father's footsteps in the study of the history of the law. I also wish to thank Professor Oliver Mitchell Wentworth Sprague, of the Graduate School of Business Administration, once Adviser to the Bank of England, for his will to help.

[71] See *Memorials of Mr. Serjeant Bellasis*, ed. 1893, p. 11, to contrast the extent of the ceremonies in 1844 with those in 1555, of which an account has been given at pages 132–136, *supra.*

PART OF A WILL

A MASSACHUSETTS mother wished to devise certain property in trust for the benefit of a daughter, A, and her issue, the trust to continue for as long a period as would be permitted under the Rule against Perpetuities. Extracts from the will which I drew to accomplish that purpose are given below.

The trustee shall invest and reinvest the trust funds; he shall collect the rents, profits, and income, deduct therefrom all expenses properly chargeable to income, and pay over the net rents, profits, and income (hereafter called the income) to my daughter A during her life.

Upon the death of A, the trust property shall be treated as belonging, absolutely or presumptively according to their age, to the issue of A then living. The trustee shall convey and pay over their shares to such issue of A as shall have reached the age of thirty years. The trust shall continue as to the shares presumptively belonging to such issue of A as shall not have reached the age of thirty years; the trustee shall pay over the income of each such share to the person to whom the share presumptively belongs, and shall convey and pay over the principal of each such share to such person, if and when he or she reaches the age of thirty years (or, if he or she dies before reaching the age of thirty years, leaving children, then to such children in equal shares).

In case any such issue of A dies before reaching the age of thirty years, leaving no children, the share of such deceased person shall then be treated as belonging, absolutely or presumptively according to their age, to the other issue of A then living. The trustee shall convey and pay over their shares of such original share to such other issue of A as shall have reached the age of thirty years. The trust shall further continue as to the shares of such original share presumptively belonging to such other issue of A as shall not have reached the age of thirty years; the trustee shall pay over the income of each such share to the person to whom the share presumptively belongs, and shall convey and pay over the principal of each such share to such person, if and when he or she reaches the age of thirty years (or, if he or she dies before reaching the age of thirty years, leaving children, then to such children in equal shares).

In any case where issue of A dies before reaching the age of thirty years, leaving no children, all shares presumptively belonging to such deceased person (whether by reason of the death of A, or by reason of one or more deaths of other issue of A) shall be disposed of, income and principal, in like manner as the share of the deceased person is disposed of under the terms of the preceding paragraph.

In case (*a*) that A shall leave no issue living at the time of her death, and in case (*b*) that issue of A shall die under the age of thirty years, leaving no children, and that there shall be no other issue of A then living, in either such case the trustee shall convey and pay over the principal to my issue then living.

Anything hereinbefore contained to the contrary notwithstanding, the trust herein provided for shall cease and determine twenty-one years after the death of the last survivor of my children and grandchildren who shall be alive at my death, and, when the trust so ceases and determines, the persons presumptively entitled under the foregoing provisions to any part of the principal, shall, by force of this provision, become absolutely entitled thereto.

A BRIEF

The Standard Cordage Company, a New York corporation, with plants in several different states, became insolvent, and Clarence H. Kelsey was appointed receiver by a New York court and was later appointed ancillary receiver of the property of the corporation in Massachusetts.

The corporation had made a mortgage to secure its bonds under which the Equitable Trust Company of New York was mortgagee, and the Trust Company retained me to foreclose the mortgage upon the Massachusetts real estate.

There was an important difference between New York and Massachusetts as to the usual method of foreclosing a mortgage. In Massachusetts, the mortgagee usually foreclosed simply by publishing in a newspaper notice of foreclosure and by having a sale pursuant to such notice; in a word, the foreclosure did *not* involve any court proceeding. But in New York there would be a court proceeding, in which there would be a foreclosure sale made by the order, under the supervision, and subject to the confirmation, of a court of competent jurisdiction.

The New York counsel for the Trust Company were keen that the foreclosure of all the plants, wherever situated, should be in court proceedings. I filed a bill in equity for the foreclosure of the mortgage upon the real estate in Massachusetts, and a single justice of the Supreme Judicial Court held that, on the special facts of the case, the court would take jurisdiction.

Now, a question arose about what would popularly be called real estate taxes. In the mortgage the corporation covenanted with the trustee to pay and discharge all taxes and assessments lawfully imposed upon the mortgaged property. Before the Trust Company took possession of the Massachusetts real estate, the City of Boston, in which city the Massachusetts real estate was situated, assessed a tax upon it and threatened to sell it for non-payment of taxes. The ancillary receiver refused to pay the tax, although he had in his hands in the Massachusetts ancillary proceedings assets more than sufficient to pay it. The Trust Company thereupon brought a bill in equity against the ancillary receiver and the Boston collector of taxes in which it prayed that the ancillary receiver might be ordered to pay the tax or that the plaintiff might pay it and be subrogated to the rights of the collector of taxes against the ancillary receiver. The ancillary receiver demurred. The demurrer was heard by a single justice of the Supreme Judicial Court who at the request of the parties sustained it *pro forma*, and reported the case for determination by the full court.

The full court overruled the demurrer. See *Equitable Trust Company of New York, trustee,* v. *Clarence H. Kelsey, receiver, and another,* 209 Mass. 416, 95 N.E. 850, Ann. Cas. 1912 B 750 (1911).

The controversy was over this question: May a real estate mortgagee require that the cumbering taxes be paid, as a preferred claim, out of the personal property of an insolvent mortgagor?

The brief filed in behalf of the Trust Company is given in full below.

SUPREME JUDICIAL COURT
FOR THE COMMONWEALTH

SUFFOLK COUNTY.   IN EQUITY.   MARCH SITTING, 1911.

THE EQUITABLE TRUST COMPANY OF NEW YORK, as Trustee,
Plaintiff,

v.

CLARENCE H. KELSEY, as Receiver of Standard Cordage Company, and BOWDOIN S. PARKER, as Collector of Taxes for the City of Boston.

BRIEF IN BEHALF OF THE PLAINTIFF UPON THE REPORT TO THE FULL COURT OF THE QUESTION WHETHER THE DEMURRER OF THE DEFENDANT KELSEY, AS RECEIVER, TO THE PLAINTIFF'S BILL SHOULD BE SUSTAINED OR OVERRULED.

Point I. A tax duly assessed to a person because of his ownership of real estate is primarily the obligation of that person. There is not even a lien upon the real estate for such tax unless given by statute. If such lien is given by statute, the nature of the tax is not changed, — the tax continues to be primarily the obligation of the person to whom it was assessed and the lien is security for that obligation.

If a tax is duly assessed to a person because of his ownership of real estate, there is no lien upon the real estate for the tax unless given by statute.

> *Dunham* v. *Lowell*, 200 Mass. 468, 469.
> Dillon, Municipal Corporations (4th ed.), sec. 821 (659).
> Cooley, Taxation (3d ed.), p. 865, note 6.

St. 1785, c. 70, provided for the assessment of property taxes, real as well as personal. The only remedies for the collection of these taxes were distress upon the goods of the person to whom they were assessed, and imprisonment of the person to whom they were assessed. There was no lien upon real estate except in special circumstances, — as where the owner was a non-resident, or became such after the assessment.

It was not until 1824 that the lien for taxes on real estate became general. St. 1823, c. 133, sec. 9. (Legislation as to Boston alone was previously enacted by St. 1821, c. 107, sec. 9.)

In *Hayden* v. *Foster*, 13 Pick. 492, 495 (1833), the effect of this legislation was before the court, and SHAW, C.J., said:

> The purpose of giving this lien seems to have been to provide a further and additional security, in the form of a real pledge for the payment of taxes on real estate. It is a remedy superadded to those of demand, distress, and imprisonment.

In *Cochran* v. *Guild*, 106 Mass. 29, the court said that the taxes on real estate might be collected otherwise than by a sale of the land. In *Roxbury* v. *Nickerson*, 114 Mass. 544, the court decided that the statutes authorizing cities to assess land for improvements (sewers) gave no remedy for enforcing such assessments except by sale of the land benefited. In the following case, *Roxbury* v. *Minot*, 114 Mass. 546, the court said, 'Taxes on real estate, being a lien on the estate, can only be enforced by a sale of the estate itself.' This remark was in no wise necessary to the decision of the question before the court. In *Swan* v. *Emerson*, 129 Mass. 289, a first mortgage on certain real estate had been given to A, and a second mortgage to B; B took possession and a tax was assessed to him on the land; A then sold, under a power of sale contained in his mortgage, to C, who paid the tax and then sought to recover the sum so paid from B. The court said, 'The taxes paid by the plaintiff, not being primarily a debt of the defendant, secured by a lien on the land, but being primarily a charge upon the land itself, the defendant is under no implied obligation to repay to the plaintiff the amount paid by him to relieve the land from that charge.' The decision in this case is clearly right. The tax was an incumbrance; C bought without any covenant against incumbrances; he presumably paid less (or, at least, the average prudent man would have paid less) because of the existence of this incumbrance; and it was unjust that he should be enriched by collecting the amount of the tax from B, — in a word, when C acquired the estate subject to the incumbrance he acquired all that he was entitled to acquire. Indeed, in *Swan* v. *Emerson*, the court proceeded to say, 'The plaintiff has no greater right of action against the defendant than any purchaser of land by a quitclaim deed, containing no covenant against incumbrances, has against his grantor for the amount of taxes previously assessed thereon to the grantor and afterwards paid by the grantee.' A similar question was presented in *Webber Lumber Co.* v. *Shaw*, 189 Mass. 366, and the court there decided the case on the ground that 'if [B] paid the tax, the lien would be discharged and [C] would hold the land free from the incumbrance, and in that way would get a greater estate in the land than that for which he paid.'

By the later cases the doctrine laid down by SHAW, C.J., in *Hayden* v. *Foster* has been established beyond peradventure.

In *Sherwin* v. *Boston Five Cents Savings Bank*, 137 Mass. 444, the dictum in *Roxbury* v. *Minot*, was criticized.

In *Richardson* v. *Boston*, 148 Mass. 508, taxes were assessed to A on certain real estate on May 1, and on May 23 the real estate was taken under an exercise of the power of eminent domain. A was held personally liable for the tax. HOLMES, J., reviewed the legislation and the decisions; pointed out that taxes on real estate are assessed, not to the estate, but 'to the person' who is owner or in possession on May 1; and adopted the language of SHAW, C.J., in *Hayden* v. *Foster*.

In *Worcester* v. *Boston*, 179 Mass. 41, 46, this doctrine was again affirmed.

In *Webber Lumber Co.* v. *Shaw*, 189 Mass. 366, the court said:

> The tax was assessed to the plaintiff as the owner of the land, and although there was a lien upon the land, the plaintiff was primarily liable for the tax. The lien on the land was simply security for its payment. As stated by SHAW, C.J., in *Hayden* v. *Foster*, 13 Pick. 492, 495, the purpose of giving such a lien 'seems to have been to provide a further and additional security in the form of a real pledge for the payment of taxes on real estate. It is a remedy superadded to those of demand, distress, and imprisonment,' and of action of contract.

In *Rogers* v. *Gookin*, 198 Mass. 434, 437, the court said:

> All taxes upon real estate are assessed, not primarily to the land, but 'to the person who is either the owner or in possession.' . . . The provision is comparatively recent, that all taxes on real estate should be a lien, distress and arrest being the early remedies.

In *Dunham* v. *Lowell*, 200 Mass. 468, the doctrine of *Hayden* v. *Foster* was again affirmed. (See also *Boston* v. *Turner*, 201 Mass. 190, 197.)

The statutes in force at the time when the tax in question was assessed, if they vary at all from the statutes construed above, reinforce the doctrine of *Hayden* v. *Foster*. (Acts 1909, c. 490, part I, secs. 15, 17; part II, secs. 21, 25, 27, 33, 36.)

Point II. If taxes are assessed to a mortgagor on real estate, and he in no wise disputes the propriety of such assessment, and he is bound by the covenants of the mortgage to pay all taxes upon the real estate, the nature of the obligation to pay such taxes, between the mortgagee and mortgagor, remains the same as it is between the mortgagor and the taxing power, — the mortgagor is primarily liable for the tax; the lien on the land is simply security for its payment; and if, for self-protection, the mortgagee is obliged to pay the tax he discharges an obligation which the mortgagor ought to have discharged.

The tax in question was assessed to the Standard Cordage Company as owner of the parcels of real estate mentioned in the bill. (Bill, paragraph sixth.) Neither the Standard Cordage Company nor the defendant Kelsey as its receiver has ever contested the propriety or validity of this assessment. (Bill, paragraph sixth.) In and by the mortgage to the plaintiff mentioned in the bill, the Cordage Company covenanted that it would 'duly pay and discharge all taxes, assessments, and governmental charges lawfully imposed upon the property and premises hereby mortgaged and pledged, or upon any part thereof, or upon the income and profits thereof, the lien of which would be prior or superior to the lien of this indenture.' (Bill, paragraph fifth.)

Land was commonly assessed to the owner until 1881. By St. 1881, c. 304, provision was made for separate assessments to the mortgagor and the mortgagee; but by St. 1882, c. 175, it was provided that, unless a certain statement were brought in, a tax to the owner should be valid. Since that time, unless such statement is brought in, the assessors continue to assess lands to the owners as they did before 1881.

> *Worcester* v. *Boston*, 179 Mass. 41, 49.
> *Abbott* v. *Frost*, 185 Mass. 398.

If the tax in question ought not to have been assessed to the Standard Cordage Company, it was for it or its receiver to establish that fact affirmatively. In *Brooks* v. *West Springfield*, 193 Mass. 190, 192, the court said:

> The mortgagor covenanted to pay all taxes that might be assessed, and the burden of proving that under R.L., c. 12, secs. 16,

17 and 18 the mortgagee's interest should have been separately
taxed was on the petitioner.

Moreover, it appears affirmatively from the allegations of the
bill that as between the mortgagor and the mortgagee this tax
ought to have been assessed precisely as it was assessed. It is a
general principle that so long as a mortgagor has the possession
and profits of real estate, it is his duty to keep down the taxes
(Jones, Mortgages (6th ed.), sec. 1080, note 325), and in the case
at bar there is an express covenant by the mortgagor to that
effect. In *Hammond* v. *Lovell*, 136 Mass. 184, the court said,
in reference to St. 1881, c. 304:

> The Legislature did not intend to interfere with or control the
> relations existing by contract between mortgagors and mortgagees.
> The plaintiff is bound by his contract, as between him and the
> mortgagee, to pay all taxes assessed upon the premises.

Acts, 1909, c. 490, part II, provides:

> Section 63. If proceedings have been commenced for the taking
> or sale of land for a tax assessed thereon, or if the owner of land has
> neglected, for three months after demand, to pay such tax, and the
> collector has made demand therefor upon the holder of a mortgage
> thereon, such holder may in like manner pay such tax, charges and
> expenses and the amount so paid may be added to the mortgage
> debt.
> Section 64. If a holder of a mortgage takes possession of land
> thereunder, all taxes due and constituting a lien thereon, and the
> expenses of any taking or sale which has been commenced or has
> taken place, may be recovered of him in an action of contract by
> the collector, or by the purchaser, as the case may be, and upon
> payment or tender by the mortgagee to the collector, or to the
> purchaser of the amounts so due within the time provided by sec-
> tion fifty-nine for owners of land to make payment, the city or town
> or the purchaser shall convey to him all the interest acquired by the
> taking or sale.

These provisions show that, as between the mortgagor and
the mortgagee, the tax is primarily the obligation of the mortgagor.

It is also to be noted that the mortgagor, upon redemption,
must pay all sums expended by the mortgagee for taxes. This
would include taxes assessed before the mortgagee took possession. (Rev. Laws, c. 187, sec. 20.)

Point III. If the mortgagee, in self-protection, is obliged to pay taxes which are an obligation of the mortgagor, he is entitled to be subrogated to all the rights of the taxing power against the mortgagor.

The mortgaged property is worth far less than the amount due under the terms of the mortgage, and the mortgagor, upon its dissolution, was hopelessly insolvent. (Bill, paragraph tenth.) If the mortgagee pays the taxes, and adds the amount so expended to the mortgage debt, the bondholders will be in no wise better off than if the mortgagee sells the property subject to the lien for the taxes, — such remedy would be a mockery.

It is the duty of the plaintiff to sell the mortgaged premises as soon as may be. If there were a sale of the mortgaged premises, subject to the lien for these taxes, the proceeds would be correspondingly diminished, and since the purchaser would have no right to have the taxes paid by the receiver (*Webber Lumber Co.* v. *Shaw*, 189 Mass. 366), the mortgagor would escape the payment of the taxes to the detriment of the holders of the bonds intended to be secured by the mortgage. For the protection of the interests of the bondholders, it is essential that the taxes be paid before the foreclosure sale. The receiver refuses to pay them. Therefore, the plaintiff, to the end that the trust reposed in it may be efficiently administered for the benefit of the bondholders, ought to make such payment now, and upon making such payment it ought to be subrogated to all the rights of the taxing power against the mortgagor.

It is submitted that the remedy given the mortgagee by statute to add the sums expended for taxes to the mortgage debt is not exclusive. These statutory provisions are permissive, not mandatory. They were designed for the protection, not the embarrassment, of the mortgagee.

The provisions of Acts 1909, c. 490, part II, secs. 63, 64, are the successors to the provisions on the same subject contained in Gen. Sts. c. 12, secs. 39, 40, 41; Pub. Sts. c. 12, secs. 52, 53, 54; St. 1888, c. 390, secs. 60, 61, 62; and Rev. Laws, c. 13, secs. 62, 63.

In *Home Savings Bank* v. *Boston*, 131 Mass. 277, 278, the court, in construing the provisions of Gen. Sts. c. 12, secs. 39, 40, 41, said:

It is true he has the right to pay the tax and to add it to the principal sum secured by his mortgage, as against the mortgagor. But he is not obliged to do so: this provision was intended for his greater security, and cannot take away or limit his right to protect his interest in any other manner.

In *Stevens* v. *Cohen*, 170 Mass. 551, 554, the court, in construing the provision of St. 1888, c. 390, secs. 60, 61, 62, said:

> The right given to the holder of a mortgage... to pay the tax, cannot be construed as interfering with his rights under the mortgage, but merely as giving an additional remedy.

In *Worcester* v. *Boston*, 179 Mass. 41, 51, the court, in construing the same provisions, said:

> We regard those provisions of the statute simply as pointing out a plain way which the mortgagee can pursue if he desires.

It is also to be noted that whereas the earlier statutes provided that the amount so paid 'shall' be added to the mortgage debt (Gen. Sts. c. 12, secs. 39, 40, 41; Pub. Sts. c. 12, secs. 52, 53, 54; St. 1888, c. 390, secs. 60, 61, 62), the later statutes provide that such amount 'may' be added to the mortgage debt (Rev. Laws, c. 13, sec. 62; Acts 1909, c. 490, part II, sec. 63).

Rev. Laws, c. 150, sec. 29, provides:

> The following claims shall, in the settlement of estates by receivers, be entitled to priority in the order named:
>
> First, debts due to the United States, or debts due to, or taxes assessed by, this Commonwealth, or a county, city, or town herein.

This gives a remedy to the taxing power for the collection of taxes (*Waite* v. *Worcester Brewing Co.*, 176 Mass. 283).

The receiver has ample funds to pay the taxes. (Bill, paragraph seventh.)

The plaintiff proposes that it should now pay the taxes, and asks that upon such payment it be subrogated to the rights of the taxing power to collect the taxes from the receiver under the provisions of this statute.

Subrogation to the rights of the tax collector was granted to the plaintiff in *Webber Lumber Co.* v. *Shaw*, 189 Mass. 366.

See also *Foote* v. *Cotting*, 195 Mass. 55.

Newell v. *Hadley*, 206 Mass. 335, 340.

The proposition that a mortgagee, who, in self-protection, pays taxes on the mortgaged premises which the mortgagor ought to have paid, is entitled, as a matter of equity (independent of any statute), to be subrogated to the rights of the taxing power against the mortgagor is abundantly supported by the authorities. (*Title Guarantee Co.* v. *Haven,* 196 N.Y. 487, 494; *Kortright* v. *Cady,* 23 Barb. 490, 497; *Eagle Insurance Co.* v. *Pell,* 2 Edw. Ch. 631, 634; *Farmer* v. *Ward,* 75 N.J.Eq. 33; *Hogg* v. *Longstreth,* 97 Penn. 255; *Ministers' Fund* v. *Folz,* 41 Pa. Super. Ct. 303; *Sharp* v. *Thompson,* 100 Ill. 447; *Pratt* v. *Pratt,* 96 Ill. 184, 194; *Bank* v. *Wyman,* 65 Kan. 314; *Lester* v. *Richardson,* 69 Ark. 198; *Childs* v. *Smith,* 51 Wash. 457; *In re Moller,* 8 Benedict, 526; Jones, Mortgages (6th ed.), sec. 358; Brant, Suretyship, sec. 353.)

The question whether a mortgagee, upon subrogation, is confined to the lien of the taxing power on the mortgaged premises (*i.e.,* whether the subrogation is only partial) has not so frequently been presented; but the language of the courts, in laying down the proposition stated in the preceding paragraph, suggests no such limitation, and, when the question has been presented, the courts have held that the mortgagee was not so confined. (*Hogg* v. *Longstreth,* 97 Penn. 255; *Ministers' Fund* v. *Folz,* 41 Pa. Super. Ct. 303; *Kortright* v. *Cady,* 23 Barb. 490, 497; *In re Moller,* 8 Benedict, 526; Jones, Mortgages (6th ed.), sec. 358.)

Jones, on Mortgages (6th ed.), sec. 358, states:

> The mortgage is usually so drawn that in terms it includes under the security any payments that may be made by the mortgagee in consequence of any default of the mortgagor. But without any such provision, the payment by the mortgagee of charges which are a prior lien, and the removal of which is essential to his own protection and safety, gives him in equity not only a right to retain the amount paid out of the proceeds of the land when sold upon foreclosure, as against the mortgagor, but also preference by way of subrogation over even prior encumbrancers who have been protected by such payment. . . .
>
> *Taxes . . . upon mortgaged lands . . . are preferred debts under the bankrupt and insolvent laws. If, therefore, such taxes and assessments be laid upon mortgaged land before the bankruptcy of the owner, they should be paid by the assignee in full out of the estate in his hands in exoneration of the mortgage.*

In re Moller, 8 Benedict, 526. A tax was assessed on real estate to the grantor, who thereafter became bankrupt. The mortgagee foreclosed and bid in the premises for less than the mortgage debt. He then applied to the bankruptcy court for a direction that the assignee pay the tax in full as a preferred claim. BLATCHFORD, J., granted the application, saying (page 531):

> By the laws of New York these taxes and assessments are made liens on the premises, prior to the liens of the mortgages, and the [mortgagee] will be obliged to pay the same before he can obtain a clear title to the premises under the foreclosure sales. The assignee has funds enough to pay these taxes and assessments in full. In opposition to this application, it is contended, for the assignee, that such taxes and assessments are a lien on the premises; that the premises are first liable for such taxes; that the mortgages were taken subject to the right to impose the taxes and assessments on the premises; that the [mortgagee] is not entitled to assert such priority in the absence of any application by the authorities of the State for the payment of such taxes and assessments out of the personal assets of the bankrupt; and that the [mortgagee] has not put in a proof of his claim.
>
> Although, for the protection of the State and to give it security for the collection of taxes and assessments, they are made liens on the premises in respect of which they are levied and made, and which are owned by the person against whom they are assessed, yet, under the laws of New York, they are personal debts of the person against whom, as owner of the premises, they are assessed. The owner of lands is assessed for the lands he owns, and the tax is imposed upon him personally, and can be collected from his property. It is, therefore, a personal debt due from him to the State for a tax or assessment. If the tax or assessment in this case be not paid, and the land be sold by the State to pay it, the sale will be a sale to satisfy a liability of the bankrupt. As the bankrupt failed to discharge this liability, and as such liability can now be discharged only by a sale of the premises, unless discharged by the assignee in full, and as such liability is made by sec. 5101 a preferred claim, and as such premises have passed into the hands of the [mortgagee], it is entirely reasonable and proper that such liability should be discharged by the assignee in full in exoneration of the premises and the [mortgagee].

Hogg v. *Longstreth*, 97 Penn. 255. A mortgaged real estate to B and then transferred the equity of redemption to C. Taxes were assessed to C as owner of the real estate. B foreclosed and bid in the property for an amount less than the mortgage debt. B was then obliged to pay the taxes assessed to C. The court held that B could recover from C the sum so paid, saying (page 259) that C was not only legally liable for the payment of the taxes, but that he had no equity for the attempt to impose payment of the taxes on another person; that by force of law the taxes were a personal charge against him, as well as a lien on the real estate; and that if B, the mortgagee, were obliged to pay the taxes for his own protection, he could look to C or to the land.

Respectfully submitted,

EDWARD H. WARREN.

WARREN, HOAGUE, JAMES & BIGELOW,
Solicitors for the Plaintiff.

Index

www.ingramcontent.com/pod-product-compliance
Lightning Source LLC
Chambersburg PA
CBHW050404110426
42812CB00006BA/1796